HISTORY, PEOPLE A
AUVERGNE

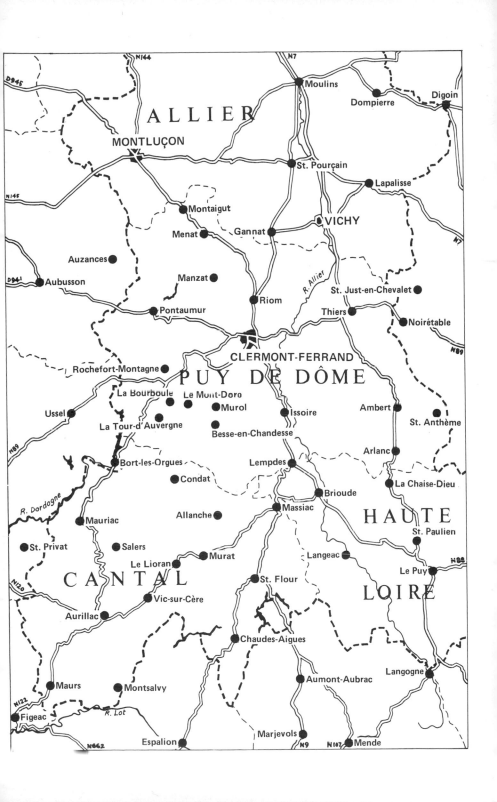

Le Château, Cordes, Puy-de-Dôme

HISTORY, PEOPLE AND PLACES IN
AUVERGNE

A. N. BRANGHAM

SPURBOOKS LIMITED

Published by Spurbooks Limited
6 Parade Court, Bourne End, Buckinghamshire

ISBN 0 904978 X

Designed and Produced by
Mechanick Exercises, London

Typesetting by Inforum, Portsmouth

Printed in Great Britain by
Chapel River Press, Andover, Hants

CONTENTS

	Illustrations	8
	Acknowledgements	10
1	Introduction to a varied province	11
2	Auvergne out of doors	17
3	The volcanic region	25
4	Hotels, food and wine	32
5	In defence of spas	42
6	From the Celts to today	49
7	Livelihood, tradition and change	63
8	Castles and churches	75
9	The Auvergnats as others see them	87
10	The makers of Auvergne	91
11	Between the Loire and Cher	104
12	Puy-de-Dome	116
13	The horizons of Velay	129
14	Cantal	144
	Bibliography	157
	Index	159

ILLUSTRATIONS

Le Château, Cordes, Puy-de-Dôme	*frontispiece*
Puy-de-Dôme	13
Besse-en-Chandesse	15
Lac Chambon, Puy-de-Dôme	18
Limayrac, Mont Dore	19
La Chataigneraie (Cantal)	20
Château ruins near the gorges de l'Allagnon (Haute Loire)	23
Volcanoes, Puy-de-Dôme	26
Plomb-du-Cantal	28
St. Flour, Les Grandes Orgues	29
Murat (Cantal)	33
A Cantal Farm	35
Crater lake, Puy-de-Dôme	36
Fromagerie at Bessé-en-Chandesse	38
Cheese-making in Auvergne	40
Le Mont Dore	44
La Bourboule — Spa resort	46
Vichy, 'Queen of Watering Places'	47
Cantal Pastures	50
St. Nectaire	54
Round Tower, Murol	55
Bourbon l'Archambault	58
Davayat, Puy-de-Dôme	60
Monument to the *Maquis*, Mont Mouchet	62
Thiers, Puy-de-Dôme	65
An Auvergnat Home	66
Auvergnat bed, Ambert	67
Lac Chambon	68
Cantal drystone *buron*	69
Folk-dance group	72
Ruins of the Château at Arlempdes	76

Château de la Barge, Puy-de-Dôme 77
Polignac, the Castle and the Church 78
The Chateau at Cordès (Puy-de-Dôme) 79
Church of Notre Dame du Port, Clermont-Ferrand 80
The Chapel of St. Michel, Le Puy 83
Auvergnat sculpture, Chapel of St. Michel 85
Issoire, Puy-de-Dôme 92
Château de Tournoel, Puy-de-Dôme 94
Château de Ravel, Puy-de-Dôme 98
Marquis d'Effiat (1581-1632) 99
Le Jacquemart, Moulins 107
The Church at Souvigny 108
The Chateau, St. Yorre 112
Hérrison, Allier 114
Thiers, the Durolle 118
Ambert 119
Orcival, Puy-de-Dôme 123
Roche Tuilière, Puy de Dôme 125
Roche Sanadoire 126
Massif Central — La Route du Sancy 128
Le Puy, Haute Loire 131
Le Puy cattle market 133
Lace-making, Le Puy 134
Approach to Pradelles in the high Cèvennes 135
La Chaise-Dieu 136
Church of St. Robert of Aurillac, La Chaise-Dieu 138
Cloister gallery, La Chaise-Dieu 139
Allègre 140
Cloisters at Lavaudieu 142
La Place, Salers, Cantal 145
La Route de Salers, Puy Mary, Cantal 146
Le Puy Mary 147
The Barrage de l'Aigle 149
La Bourrée, St. Flour, Cantal 151
Garabit Viaduct, Cantal 152
Chaudes-Aigues 155

Acknowledgements

I am happy to record my gratitude to Professor Glyn Daniel, Litt. D., F.S.A. for enlightening a layman over the problems connected with the dating of the 'prehistoric' finds at Glozel (Allier). His lucid explanation has been incorporated into Chapter 11, and any errors or misinterpretations in it are my responsibility, certainly not his.

The book's illustrations have been supplied by the always helpful French Government Tourist Office in London.

1

INTRODUCTION TO A VARIED PROVINCE

In the days before the universality of the motor car had dissolved the Frenchman's indifference to anything outside his own region, many a non-Auvergnat was unsure where the province of Auvergne lay. So there is no need for an English reader similarly unsure, to feel that his education has been defective.

As far as this book is concerned (which means that other writers may disagree), Auvergne consists of the four *départements* of Allier, Puy-de-Dôme, Haute-Loire and Cantal. It needs three Michelin maps (on a scale of one cm to two km), 69, 73 and 76, to encompass this area.

Between them, the four *départements* form the northern segment of the huge upland area that covers some 55,000 square km, and is known as the Massif Central. The name implies that those uplands lie in the centre of the hexagon of France. They do not. The Massif Central lies almost wholly in southern France, for its most southerly tip in Aveyron in the Cévennes is no more than 50 km as the crow flies from the Mediterranean Sea near Montpellier. Nonetheless, this mountain barrier, west of the river Rhône, gives the feeling of being the centre of France, holding apart the lowland plains of northern France and the Mediterranean shore; an upland fulcrum balancing north and south, the two geographical, climatic, demographic and cultural opposites of France. Auvergne, climatically, leans to the north; linguistically, to the south.

The actual geographical centre of France is marked on one of the roads entering Auvergne from the north. Thirty-six km out of Bourges on the Montluçon road is Bruère-Allichamps. A Roman milestone in the centre of the quaint town marks a supposed geographical centre of France, though the stele is not quite where the Romans had put it. More recent calculations have placed the 'true' centre at Saulzais-le-Potier, twenty-five km. further south but still in the Cher *département*; another commune, that of Vesdun, also claims the honour.

Wherever this notional geographical centre may be, Auvergne begins south of it. Can we say that Auvergne is not *at* the centre of France, but *in* the centre of France? For Auvergne begins south of the 'true' centre, with the *département* of Allier. Its most southerly *département* is Cantal. I can think of little that unites the two, save their greenness, for Auvergne is a province of disparate elements.

Tourist publicity makes much of the volcanic hills of Auvergne. There is much more to Auvergne than just the 'burnt region', as the historian, Jules Michelet, put it. Diversity, rather than homogeneity is its attraction. Only part of the province is occupied by the volcanic zone. Wide and fertile plains, forests and stony plateaux, sudden valleys and unexpected lakes, hillshapes sharp with glacial grinding or smoothly and softly folded. There are strange shapes, as though devised by ingenuity rather than accident — the organpipe basalt rocks or the termitary stacks of volcanic rock. Little villages, solid and satisfied farmsteads, decay and revival among the wind-blown horizons. Differing shapes of buildings, differing patterns of agriculture dictated here by alluvium, there by granite or sedimentary rock; dry areas and wet ones. Distinctive terrains labelled by ancient names — Limagne, Forez, Combrailles, Arlense, Margeride, Livradois, Velay, Bois Noirs, Monts de la Madeleine, Cézallier or Châtaigneraie. A composite land whose various fragments will be visited as the book progresses.

This wrinkled and pummelled landscape is crossed by only one low-numbered *Route Nationale*, RN9 from Paris, through Clermont-Ferrand, Auvergne's capital, on its way towards Spain. RN7 flicks briefly through the north-east corner between Moulins and Lapalisse, on the Paris — Lyon — Côte d'Azur highway. Mineral resources are not great enough to have attracted vast industrial enterprises. Much of Auvergne has had a tradition of poverty, with small, scattered communities. For the traveller, the natural barriers of Auvergne have held back excessive urban expansion. It is a land which does not lend itself to the rationalisation dear to the heart of administering plainsmen. Its hills, none of which reach even 2,000 metres, are high enough to slow progress and time, while yet providing well-engineered even if sometimes slow and narrow roads. In the uplands there is a quality of remoteness, a fastness, as one English writer has called it; a haunted land, in the thought of another.

English writers have not, I think, entered into passionate love relations with Auvergne. Unlike Provence, whose Mediterranean classicism is redolent of our civilisation's origins, Auvergne presents — in its uplands, at least — a landscape which makes history irrelevant even though traditions endure. It is an astringent personality which commands our respect.

Regional authors, however, have written impassioned passages about their native soil. For them, Auvergne is an incomparable paradise, an entrancing fairyland, a world where every colour of the artist's palette is brushed upon every dawn and sunset, where everything is touched with noble eloquence, antique beauty, wisdom and romantic melancholy as of the angelus. Perhaps I parody a little. But such high-pitched writing, music to French ears, is usually beyond the range of English hearing. Such unreal melodrama did come from

12

Puy-de-Dôme

the pen of Jean Ajalbert (1863-1947) in his *Au Coeur de l'Auvergne*. It is a measure of his regional attachment, and, perhaps, of his Celtic origin, and speaks of the comparative isolation Auvergne has both enjoyed and suffered down the years.

However Auvergne is described, it is difficult to do justice to a province which can claim as much variety as any in France. No single descriptive caption can span these diversities, though one such did catch my eye. Local public relations writers tried their muse hard to come up with the eyebrow-raising ambiguity of 'Land of fecundity, land of beauty, land of health!'

*   *   *

An idiosyncratic pleasure of travelling in France is to note the ancient names of regions still in daily use, even though they have had no official recognition for nearly a couple of centuries, when the French Revolution banished the reminders of regal and ducal possessions and fiefdoms. Auvergne's name is no exception, although its origins go back almost to the edge of written European history. It derives, little changed, from the original inhabitants, the Arverni, those Celtic Auvergnats Caesar had some trouble in quelling.

Between Montluçon and Moulins in Allier lies the aristocratic-sounding Bourbonnais — the first Sires of Bourbon came from Bourbon-l'Archambault, also in Allier, to give their name to the royal house of France, as ancestors to the kings of France from Henri IV on.

Auvergne's eastern flank bears the old names of Velay and Forez. The people of Velay are the Vellaves; again, the modern equivalent of the Celtic tribe of Vellavi who sided with the Arverni against the Romans.

Other ancient names encircle Auvergne. To the north is fertile Berry, the outer rim of the Paris Basin. Then, anticlockwise, follow Limousin, Périgord, Quercy, Ségalas and Rouergue whose limestone tablelands are the summer pastures for sheep. The *département* of Cantal is bounded by granitic Gévaudan whose name still has a faintly sinister ring. Between 1764 and 1766 Gévaudan was terrorised by a marauding wolf which devoured nearly seventy shepherdesses and their children before it was despatched by the king's best marksman. For nearly a century afterwards, wolves were still feared in Gévaudan, and their awfulness was perpetuated in literature. Then comes Vivarais (today's Ardèche) which faces the Rhône and gives the first real hint of the Mediterranean. Then Beaujolais and Burgundy, neither ever in danger of obscurity as long as wine is reverenced, and, to complete the cycle beyond the Auvergne perimeter, Berry again.

In up-to-date terms, Allier's main towns are Moulins, Montluçichy, Lapalisse, St. Pourçain-sur-Sioule and Bourbon-l'Archambault. Puy-de-Dôme, the central *département* of the province, has Clermont-Ferrand as capital at its heart, Issoire, Ambert and Thiers, St. Eloy-les-Mines and Riom, and the bulk of Auvergne's spas, such as Châtel-Guyon, Royat and St. Nectaire, La Bourboule and Le Mont Dore. The capital of Cantal is Aurillac, with the major towns of Mauriac, St. Flour and Chaudes-Aigues in a thinly populated region. Finally, to the east is Haute-Loire, spread around celebrated Le Puy; Yssingeaux, Brioude and La Chaise-Dieu are the other towns of any consequence.

Auvergne tilts towards the west in the geographical, demographical and industrial sense. To its south and east rise the steep barrier ridges of the Cévennes, the outer wrapping of the Massif Central. But in the opposite direction the land inclines towards Atlantic Aquitaine. Auvergne was once part of the English domain of Aquitaine, and it still belongs to Atlantic France which is industrially poorer, with fewer natural resources, is more sparsely populated and lacks commercial communications compared with continental France. This is why Auvergne tends to look towards the rural past, towards the outer margin furthest away from the powerhouses and initiatives of 20th century France.

Most of the major rivers flow towards the rich open plains of the Aquitanian Basin. 'The water tower of France', the Massif Central has been called. The

Besse-en-Chandesse

Hérault rises there and flows into the Mediterranean; the Gard and Ardèche are short and course rapidly into the Rhône. The Tarn, Viaur, Aveyron, Lot, Truyère and Dordogne all flow west towards the Atlantic's Bay of Biscay. The almost 1,000 kilometre long Loire and its tributaries, the Allier and Cher, plus the Dore and Sioule which both rise and join the Allier in Auvergne, all steer a northerly course before the Loire swings west through the château country and out to sea as the southern boundary to Brittany.

Into these rivers run small tributaries, dozens of them. They have carved out for themselves innumerable lateral valleys, stamping their character on the crumpled landscape to make of Auvergne a canoeist's and fisherman's playground.

The position and direction of all the important valleys of the Massif Central bear on regional climates. Auvergne is the mixing bowl for France's three climatic influences. First, the Mediterranean — hot, dry, cloudless summers, mild, bright winters and regular seasonal rainfall. Although barred by the Cévennes and other hills on the right bank of the Rhône, the Mediterranean climate breaks through on the hot, humid, south or southeast winds that melt the winter snows of Auvergne and put the rivers in spate, and inflict the thunderstorms of summer.

15

Second, and most dominant, is the Atlantic climate, particularly during summer. West or southwest winds prevail, bringing soft rain and a slow onset of seasons, to produce cool summers and mild winters in the easily penetrated east-west facing valleys. North-south ranges hold back the Atlantic climate, and their valleys are more influenced by the third climatic pattern, the continental.

Cold winters and warm, long summers which are often thundery, are characteristics of the great continental landmass of Europe. This climatic pattern peters out in Burgundy and around Lyon, but enters the wide basins of the Loire and Allier to give warm, dry summers, cold winters and low rainfall.

Outside the Bourbonnais, Auvergne has all the ingredients of an unpredictable mountain climate. Winds blow at cross-purposes, and day-to-day predictions demand a nice balance between confidence and escape clauses. Different patterns of rainfall and temperature, of sunshine and cloud, are noticeable within short distances. Relief and altitude play their crucial roles. But the expectation of sunshine is higher than with other mountain ranges because many Auvergnat valleys are broad. Only very general distinctions can be made. In the uplands over 1,000 metres, winters are long and hard; snowfall is heavy. Hence the development of winter sports notably cross-country skiing. North winds produce deep drifts, and winter lingers late into spring on the heights. Average annual rainfall there is over 1.5 metres. By contrast, Clermont-Ferrand, at an altitude of 400 metres and at the edge of the fertile Limagne, has an annual rainfall of only 500 mm.

On the Puy-de-Dôme (1,465 metres) outside Clermont-Ferrand, can be witnessed the phenomenon of temperature inversion. When it is freezing hard in Clermont itself, the mountain-top temperature can be as much as 20° C. higher, as cold, heavy layers of air slip down into the valley, pushing up the warm air from below. In late autumn, the top of the Puy-de-Dôme and other hills in the chain can be bathed in brilliant sunshine, each height seeming to stand as an isolated hump upon an eiderdown of dense cloud which is smothering the Limagne valley.

To tour Auvergne in May and June is to see the contrast between snow on the higher slopes and the warmth of the open valleys with their spring flowers and fruit trees in blossom. High summer, hot and dry in the valleys, is fresh and invigorating in the hills, a weather pattern which can be continued into autumn with the leaf-change, while the valleys begin to collect the mists as the days draw in.

A little piece of advice, then, to visitors to Puy-de-Dôme, Cantal and Haute-Loire: always carry clothing which anticipates the probability of sharp fluctuations in temperature in the same place, even in July and August.

2

AUVERGNE OUT OF DOORS

Above all, Auvergne is rural. Everything manmade is put in place by the wide and often empty landscapes. From them stem the natural resources the active visitor will want to enjoy.

As this is the water-tower of France, it is sensible to look first at the water courses. Broad, gentle and poplar-lined, the river Allier flows through Vichy to be fully exploited by the resort. On the banks of the river is a vast sporting complex: sports club, race course, golf course, tennis courts, swimming pool, and riverside beaches. This is one of the finest nautical centres in France for sailing, water-skiing, rowing, canoeing. By damming the river, the Lac d'Allier has been created to give still more space to water sports. All very sophisticated, gregarious and international, and, no doubt, not cheap. No image here of the genteel, decrepit hypochondriacs who are supposed to sip the horrid waters at the spa — but more of that in a later chapter.

Some of the natural lakes — such as Lacs d'Aydat, Chambon, Guéry, Pavin and St. Bonnet — are used for sailing, swimming or canoeing. Water sports are also practised on the artificial reservoirs — Barrages de Besserve, Bort, Brommat, Grandval, Lavalette, Sarrans and St. Etienne-Cantalès.

Canoe-kayaking enthusiasts have a choice of both easy and difficult courses. Lakes and reservoirs are the simplest, of course, but so too are the Allier and the lower reaches of the Sioule. Difficult courses can be undertaken, as a rule, only between January and the end of March when the water levels are adequate and the weather is cold. The upper Sioule, Couze, Allanche, Alagnon and Dore rivers are all classified as difficult for light craft.

Every kind of river fishing is to be had, from mountain torrents to slow, plateau-streams. Each *département* has an official fishing society which willingly provides information.

Salmon fishing in the Allier is a major attraction. The fish make their way upstream, and three zones and periods are recognised. Between Châtel-de-Neuve and Vichy the season is roughly between mid-January and February. The middle zone is between Maringues and Issoire, with fishing in March and April. Finally, between Brioude and Langeac, the salmon season is in May and June.

Lac Chambon, Puy-de-Dôme

The trout season is from mid-February to late September, the main period being between the end of March and the end of June. There are plenty of trout streams at all altitudes.

The white fish season is from 1st January to 28th February, and from 15th June to 31st December. Bleak, dace, chub, gudgeon, barbel, perch and roach are usually fished with gentles, and are found in swift, shallow rivers. Pike are common in rivers, lakes and reservoirs. There are three fishing seasons in the year, the chief one being from 1st September to 30th November.

*   *   *

As far as winter sports are concerned, Auvergne is still something of a poor relation compared with the glamour of the alpine slopes of Savoy and Provence, and its resources are rather more modest than those in the Pyrenees. Nevertheless, there are many well established centres especially for cross-country skiing, *ski de fond*. Le Mont Dore (1,050m - 1,846m) and Super-Besse (1,350m - 1,850m) are both equipped with cable-cars and hoists, ski-schools and hotels. Both are in Puy-de-Dôme.

18

Challenging them is Cantal's Super-Lioran (1,153 — 1,850m); then come more modest centres such as St. Anthème and Tour d'Auvergne. Still less familiar are Les Estables in Haute-Loire at the foot of Mont Mézenc (1,754m) with a population of under 700 and a handful of small and modest hotels. Anzat-le-Luguet on the Cézallier slopes began life as a ski resort in 1970. Le Brugeron in the Monts du Forez, Chastreix in the Sancy massif, and Picherande which specialises in cross-country skiing are struggling to put themselves on the winter sports map. In Allier, there are hotel-less centres at Laprugne and St. Nicolas-des-Biefs, both in the Montagne Bourbannaise, where the only accommodation is in lodgings, the *gîtes ruraux*. Anyone looking for something really off the map, and offering, perhaps, a little ski oneupmanship, may care to investigate the hamlet of La Loge-des-Gardes, at 1,077m in the Monts de la Madeleine, still hardly mentioned by guide books.

* * *

Limayrac, Mont Dore

La Chataigneraie (Cantal)

Nature designed Auvergne to be a walking country, although cycling holidays there are beginning to return to favour. Some easy hill-walking inclusive tours are arranged by tour operators in Britain who offer two-centre holidays at Le Falgoux and St. Julien-de-Jordanne; St. Anthème and St. Jacques-des-Blats; or single centre holidays at places such as Le Chambon.

There are many villages from which one can set out for longer or shorter excursions on foot. For those with strong legs who set their sights on longer walks, there are marked paths (usually indicated by red and white signs) across country of varying difficulty through the length and breadth of France. These are the *Sentiers de Grande Randonnée,* administered by a central organisation in Paris which publishes walking maps or *topoguides* for the various regions, leaflets giving advice on equipment and preparation, and a quarterly magazine.

Auvergne has a network of such paths that cross some of the loveliest sections of countryside. Only some of them are indicated on the Michelin maps by a broken black line with 'GR' followed by the route number.

GR4, when completed, will cross France from Cannes on the Côte d'Azur to

20

Royan on the Atlantic coast. It crosses Auvergne from St. Flour, over the Plomb du Cantal and Puy Mary summits, past Lac Chauvet, over the Chaîne des Puys and Puy de Dôme to swing west towards Aubusson.

GR41 is being worked on, and is to go from Mont Pilat to the Loire at Tours; its Auvergne section is between Le Puy-en-Velay, Brioude, Super-Besse, beyond which it meets the completed GR33, running eastwards between Olliergues and Crocq in Creuse. At Olliergues it descends to the Dore valley at Pont de Longues, goes to the old Celtic site at Gergovie, then to Ceyrat, Pontaumur on the Sioule, where it meets up with GR4. GR331 is an alternative route which runs south of the Gergovie plateau.

GR3 follows much of the Loire valley from near the source of the river, through Le Puy to St. Bonnet, to cross the cols of Monts du Forez to Lapalisse and Dompierre-sur-Besbre.

GR65 heads southwest from Le Puy over the Monts du Velay and Margeride to link up with GR4; its projected continuation is to the great church of Conques.

For rock-climbing of various grades of difficulty Auvergne has a number of challenging sites — Boisséjour, Gorges de la Bourne, Enval, Chaudefour are examples—and the *Section d'Auvergne* of the *Club Alpin Français* has its headquarters in Clermont-Ferrand. Subterranean climbing is catered for by the *Groupe spéléologique Auvergnat* in Clermont-Ferrand, and one of the most interesting of caves is the Creux de Soucy near Lac Pavin. The limestone cave systems of the Grands Causses lie a little outside Auvergne.

While horses can be hired for riding at any number of centres, some English tour operators have planned inclusive riding holidays with tuition in the Massif Central.

*   *   *

Naturalists are less impressed by arbitrary political boundaries than by ecological unities. Consequently, naturalists will prefer to consider the Massif Central as a whole rather than the confines of our four *départements.* To the flower-lover not over-concerned with the scientific niceties of microhabitats, plant communities or precise nomenclature, the lowland roadsides and meadows in May and June are sheer delight. Not that the flowers there are rare varieties, but because of the brilliant mosaic of colour, whether of the fields of narcissi, the sheets of forget-me-nots, cranesbills, saxifrages, globe flowers, honeysuckle, marsh marigolds, or even the garden flowers. An early autumn delight, especially in Cantal and Haute-Loire, is the sight of thousands of autumn crocuses pushing their delicate lilac petals through the short, strong turf of acres and acres of pasture.

To such visual delights are added the discreet sounds of nature behind the great silences that accompany the Cantalian countryside in particular. A cry of a bird, the squeak of voles; in spring, the meadows ring with the cheerful rasp of crickets, and again in late summer; in high summer, grasshoppers stridulate their love melodies and combat calls.

For the systematic botanist, the Massif Central's diversity of landform and ecological niches make for sustained interest. Four different elements impinge themselves and bring with them characteristic plant communities. In the Cévennes and southern Cantal, the Mediterranean element puts in a tentative appearance, as can be seen by the frequency of holm oak and scrubland up to 500m or more. Above this is the sweet chestnut zone; a whole area of Cantal is known as La Châtaigneraie, a lightly populated part of unproductive granite uplands whose valleys produce the chestnuts. Maurs is the centre, and it is sometimes referred to as the 'Riviera of Cantal', where vines and Mediterranean plants — figs, pomegranates and cactus — grow here and there.

The Central European element is characterised by silver fir and beech forests, particularly on the ridges of the Forez and Madeleine hills up to 1,000m. Higher still come the high pastures known as the Hautes Chaumes. Where the micro-climate is relatively sunny and dry Scots pines attain a fair stature in the ravines.

Then there is the Atlantic element of cool, moist summers and mild, wet winters in the lower regions, and snow in the mountains. Where one sees the wide and luminous Auvergnat heathlands, there the Atlantic climate dominates, and the outstanding plants are lilac- or white-flowered Cornish heath, and Spanish gorse.

The fourth element is the Boreal in which arctic-alpine species flourish. Many parts of the region are natural rock gardens with a profusion of mountain species which are the delight of all flower lovers. These rock gardens begin to appear at around 1,200m, lower than you would find their counterparts in the Alps or Pyrenees, on account of the abundant summer rainfall brought in by the Atlantic winds. The volcanic mountains show the alpine plants at their best.

The alpine pastures lie beyond the limit of the forests. They are either natural or man created through fire and felling which has gone on down the centuries, but particularly during the French Revolution. No wonder the Massif Central is sometimes referred to as 'the bald pate of France'. Up in these pastures a rich and colourful variety of mountain flowers appears towards the end of June. All kinds of anemone and pulsatilla, globe flowers, saxifrages, stonecrops, mountain avens, daffodils, pheasant's-eye narcissus, bluebells, broom, dwarf willow, alpine clover, rock jasmine, arnica, whorled solomon's seal, marsh gentians and great yellow gentians, martagon lilies, wild angelica, alpine violets and pansies. There is also the alpine mouse-eared chickweed, notable for the fact it is also recorded from the northernmost botanical locality in the world. And, as the snows retreat, so the crocuses, snowdrops and jonquils emerge.

Of a more recondite interest are the plants which normally grow by the sea or in salt marshes. They find the mineral springs of Auvergne congenial; they include such species as the greater sea spurrey and sea milkwort.

One of the best-known botanical areas is on the slopes of the Puy de Sancy (1,886m) above Super-Besse. Lower down, at Besse-en-Chandesse, is a biological laboratory of the University of Clermont-Ferrand, where local fauna and flora are studied.

In this very brief botanical survey, let us not omit those essential adjuncts to gastronomy, the mushrooms. The sequence of appearance of edible fungi in Auvergne is roughly: morel, fairy-ring champignon, chanterelle, the cep or *Boletus edulis*, saffron milk cap, parasol mushroom, wood blewit, and blue leg blewit.

* * *

Compared with some other bird-watching areas of France, the Massif Central is not so well known. According to John Gooders, Cantal has worthwhile districts. He gives St. Flour as a suitable centre. Certainly, St. Flour is attractive in its own right, strikingly perched on a great escarpment, and well supplied with tourist facilities. Nearly ten km north of the town, on the Clermont-Fer-

Château ruins near the gorges de l'Allagnon (Haute Loire)

rand road, is Col de la Fageole (1,104m). This, says Gooders, is an excellent place from which to look out for birds of prey — Red Kite, Montagu's Harrier, Booted Eagle, Buzzard, as well as Cirl Bunting. Another noted raptor area, further north on the same road, is Lempdes, where the Gorges d'Alagnon broaden out, and the riverside woodlands are full of small birds such as Red-backed Shrike, Wryneck, Cirl Bunting and other small passerines. The third area Gooders mentions is the wooded hills around the artificial reservoir of Garabit, in the far south of Cantal. Crested tit, Black Restart, Short-toed Tree-creeper, Firecrest and Woodchat Shrike are to be found in the vicinity.

* * *

Suffice it to say that, as far as butterflies and moths are concerned, Auvergne is rich in species through the diversity of habitats. Of special interest to the northerner who comes from the lowlands are both the alpine, as well as the Mediterranean species which have infiltrated into the warmer outer rim of the Massif Central. There are also those species which breed and survive locally, cut off from the Alps and Pyrenees to give rise to intricate questions of distribution, spread, number of broods, foodplants and subspecies.

A few examples of butterfly curiosities can be mentioned to whet the lepidopterist's appetite.

The Poplar Admiral, for example is at its southwest European limit in Auvergne. The Cranberry Fritillary is to be found only in the boggy areas where the larval footplant is confined. The genetically variable Heath Fritillaries produce two subspecies, one on each side of a 'frontier' which crosses the Massif Central from east to west. A subspecies to be hemmed in on the grassy slopes above 1,300m is the Ottoman Brassy Ringlet which flies in July. Smaller and paler varieties of the Autumn Ringlet occur in Lozère. The Violet Copper is probably confined to the damp meadows of Monts Dore; this species exists only in scattered colonies in western Europe, its larva feeding on knot grass. Another butterfly that is restricted to the southern part of the Massif Central is a subspecies of the Furry Blue, here slightly smaller and darker than the species.

But for less specialised pleasure there are plenty from among the 380 species of European butterfly, from the showy Swallowtails to the little Skippers, to be observed and admired.

The same is true of the moths, from the great furry flutterings around some street lamp of the Wild Silk Moths, and the sombre hues of the Death's Head Hawk Moth — and the many other hawk moths, of which the most enchanting is always the elfin flash from flower to flower of the day-flying Humming Bird Hawk Moth — down to the countless nondescript microlepidoptera.

May I invite every visiting naturalist to respect the diversity of wild life by observing it, not collecting it? Please leave this habitat as you found it.

3

THE VOLCANIC REGION

Best known of all Auvergne's outdoor attractions — and therefore demanding a chapter to themselves — are the extinct volcanoes. 'An extraordinary natural museum', is how the great vulcanologist, Haroun Tazieff, has called them. These dormant volcanoes have made Auvergne unique in Europe. They have given rise to a remarkable landscape; they have determined much of the architecture and sculpture in it; they have imposed a particular character on towns within range of their influence. In order to preserve the region a Volcano Park has been decreed, or, to give it its full title (and in France a long title is preferred when a short one would do), *Le Parc Naturel Régional des Volcans d'Auvergne.*

The Park is divided into two separated sections. The northern part is an irregular elongation west of Clermont-Ferrand, stretching from its tip at Charbonnières-les-Vieilles to just south of Aydat. In an area about 35km by 16km it takes in the Chaîne des Puys range — also known as the Monts Dômes — itself part of the larger Monts d'Auvergne.

The southern section of the Park lies in Cantal, with the towns of Vic-sur-Cère and Murat lying at opposite points of a circumference which encircles the Massif des Plombes. Separating the two sections of the Park are the Monts Dore and Monts du Cézallier, the latter a granite plateau overlaid with basalt lava, a beautiful area of pasturelands.

Having undergone different geological experiences at different times, the two sections of the Volcano Park are totally dissimilar in appearance. The northern Chaîne des Puys comprises no less than sixty well-defined cones. Those that are smooth-domed are composed of acid lava; those with craters are of basalt. Some of the hills are denuded; others are covered by forests planted, for the most part, during the last century. Strung out over 35km, the high point is the Puy-de-Dôme (1,465m), overlooking Clermont-Ferrand. From its summit is the classic panorama of the whole chain.

Strewn about, as though placed with care by some hand are, one could imagine, the softly rounded forms of potter's clay, stretching away into the distance. An obsessive fancy for cones and cupolas, sometimes scored up their

Volcanoes, Puy-de-Dôme

sides, seems to have motivated the potter. Here the cone is depressed by a light pressure of his thumb; there a finger has begun to shape a whorl. Or else, losing patience, he has brushed down the side of a crater, like the Puys of Lassolas and Vache whose collapsed valleys gave rise to lakes such as those of Aydat and Cassière, and whose molten lava had burned the trees to form the wood-coal below the basalt layers.

The geological complexities of the region are for the specialists to whom the different kinds of molten matter extruded have profound significances, and which give rise to a whole hermetic language. The Puy-de-Dôme, they say, is the only cone known to have extruded 'plastic' lava, a thick, grey silica called trachyte. Some domes, like those of Sarcoui, Chaudron and Clierzon, emitted a viscous lava which gave the cupola effect; or the uplifted granite block of Puy Chopine whose lava was solid.

These blisters on the burned surface of the earth's skin have hardly changed since they erupted and poured black and disorderly lava to form the *cheires* in the high plateau above which most of the summits rise a mere few hundred metres. They are very young. One carbon-14 dating indicates their period of eruption to have been between 8,000 and 10,000 years ago. The most senior of them is Gravenoire, east of the main group. But there are other estimates.

80,000 years for the oldest volcano in the region of Mauzat, while others were still active between 6,000 and 6,500 years ago, with the last eruption of Puy de Montcineyre in 1,500 B.C., during the Bronze Age.

As you approach Clermont-Ferrand from Riom, and glance westwards, these humps stand, well spaced, rounded, tranquil. From below they do not look dramatic, but they impart a measured beauty as backcloth to the valley.

Glacial erosion never touched the smooth hillocks of the Chaîne des Puys, but it did the Monts du Cantal, the southern section of the Volcano Park. Their present-day physiognomy betrays the experience. In the Tertiary period they had formed a huge volcano, larger by far than any other in Europe. This volcano had been 3,000m high which erosion has reduced to a series of apparently unrelated peaks of varying shapes. The highest, the Plomb du Cantal (1,855m) is rounded; Puy Mary is pyramidal; Puy Griou is needle-shaped. Originally, the cone reached from the Plomb du Cantal to the Puy Violent, with Puy Griou at its heart. The landscape is dramatic. Deep valleys radiate from the centre of the one-time crater, and arrowhead peaks, the residue of solidified lava, and the outlying inclines formed by lava-flows (the *planèzes*) make up fertile pasture and agricultural land. The active cone had covered an area of 2,700 square km, and had an elliptical base of 240km; it erupted for about twenty million years.

As with other regional parks in France, the Auvergne Volcano Park has numerous objectives. The overriding wish is to preserve the countryside; its unusual geological features; its natural contents of plant, animal, bird and insect life and their habitats; and the residual forests. Of special interest to naturalists is the preservation of the mountain boglands. Nature reserves are to be created within the Park so that biological phenomena peculiar to the region can be studied. On the human level, fresh social and economic impetuses are needed in an area poor in natural resources and which has experienced many years of depopulation.

For the temporary visitor, the opening up, signposting and maintenance of footpaths, is a primary concern. This programme is being developed, even if only slowly; there are maps and guides — in particular, the *topoguides* I have already mentioned. Regional ethnic museums showing the traditional forms of husbandry are planned. Care is being taken over the recreational equipment on and around the lakes, so as to avoid over-development. Also on the drawing-board are new holiday villages, *villages de vacances*.

There are no formal boundaries or fences, neither entrance gates nor charges. You merely enter an area, here and there signposted, and marked on some maps to designate a conservation region, the concept for which arose out of the needs and wishes of the local populace. The organisation, too, is essentially local. Quite simply, the Park is where anyone can enjoy nature without the dangers of encroachment by industry and urban expansion. I dare say it will fall short of the original ideals; but it is a worthwhile project, nonetheless.

Plomb-du-Central

Other volcanic mountains exist in Auvergne outside the Park. West of the Chaîne des Puys are eighty basalt craters in the Sioule valley, though largely eroded away. In the Limagne plain, east and southeast of Clermont-Ferrand, are a number of strange-looking rocks, such as Puy de Crouel, Buttes de Cournon, Lempdes, Pont-du-Château and Vertaizon. These shapes were produced when the Limagne was a lake, and the hot lava was turned into powder on contact with water and mud, more than thirty million years ago. Another volcanic group in the Limagne is of basalt — black lava of silica mixed with chalk — which was active between ten and twenty million years ago. With them, the lava flowed over clay and limestone to create the plateau-tops of Gergovie, Chanturge, Châteaugay, Corent and the Côtes de Clermont-Ferrand.

One of the largest volcanoes in Europe is the Massif du Mont-Dore which ejected some 250 cubic km of cinders and lava over a surface of 600 square km. This is an area six times greater than that of Vesuvius. Not only was it covered, between one and four million years ago, with layers of volcanic detritus, it was also bombarded with huge volcanic hailstones. The volcanic cones of the Massif du Cézallier, between Mont-Dore and Cantal, have long since been

St. Flour, Les Grandes Orgues

levelled by erosion into a great granite tableland overlaid with basalt and quiet pastures.

Between Billom and Vic-le-Comte in Puy-de-Dôme is the volcanic group known as les volcans du Comte d'Auvergne, its worn down mounds having once served as eminently suitable sites for now ruined castles.

A little further afield, in Velay and Vivarais (the latter strictly outside Auvergne), are the three volcanic ranges of Devès, Mégal and Mézenc which

29

erupted between one and two million years ago. The basalt lava gave rise to the spendid organpipe structures in the landscape; the phonolite lava giving birth to the *sucs* of viscous lava of the Gerbier des Joncs, where the Loire rises, and the Mézenc.

Round Le Puy are the dramatic volcanic needles or *dykes*, such as the much-photographed Rochers Corneille and d'Aiguilhe, residual hard cores of eroded cones.

If the dormant volcano world poses problems for the geologist, it also is a happy hunting ground for the amateur mineralogist. A profusion of semi-precious stones, offspring of volcanic upheavals, can be found. Some of them are exploited commercially or industrially. Pozzolana cement is quarried at Gravenoire above Royat, and in Royat itself are lapidary workshops and a permanent exhibition of gemstones. The open quarries of Volvic have for long extracted andesite, a very hard lava out of which the Michelin signposts throughout France used to be made. Le Puy de Beaunit is a centre for fine olivines which are used both as gemstones as well as for industrial moulding. Greenish zircons, soft red garnets, amethysts, topaz, beryl, fluorite — the latter once an ornamental stone, now used in steel-making — are but some of the more familiar gemstone names which occur, sometimes commonly, sometimes as rareties, in Auvergne. Of the chalcidony varieties, banded agates are mined. So, too, is hematite, often seen in signet rings and cuff-links.

*   *   *

Only in more recent years have the dynamics of mountain building and volcano formation been clearly perceived. Today, the theory of continental drift is widely accepted. It had been advanced at the beginning of this century but regarded with scepticism until the last fifteen years. Floating on the semifluid mantle of the earth is the apparently hard and immovable crust of granite rocks, sometimes spoken of as 'sial', which underlie the visible landscape. In fact, this crust is composed of plates many miles thick which float imperceptibly on a basaltic layer or 'sima'. Together, the layers form a thickness of some forty km, and float on the 2,900 km thickness of mantle. They are carried by convection currents. The plates, on which the continents rest, collide, forcing other plates upwards or downwards. Stresses build up at these areas of contact, and the rock crust splits and releases the molten material imprisoned below which emerges through the vents or conduits of the classical volcano.

The Massif Central had formed part of a V-shaped chain of mountains, the Hercynian Chain, across northern France. During the Tertiary period, the process of alpine folding fractured the hard rock to create two lines of weakness that followed the valleys of the Allier and the Loire. These splits went deep into the earth's mantle and created the conditions by which volcanoes could become active. But it so happened that the continental drift stopped where Auvergne now lies. The rifts have healed over, and earthquakes and volcanic eruptions have long since been stilled.

Life of the distant past lies fossilised below in volcanic dusts and once molten lava. Extinct mammals — sabre-toothed tigers and mastodons among them — forests and trees that grew when the climate was different from today's, have been embalmed in the tranquil countryside by sustained holocausts in the geological past.

4

HOTELS, FOOD AND WINE

In the field of tourism, Auvergne is a johnny-come-lately which has had to live down a reputation for poor hotels and rough food. The notion derives from vague recollections of Auvergne's past poverty and inaccessibility. People have imagined inns to be as unsavoury as Robert Louis Stevenson sometimes found them during his travels with a donkey through the Cévennes in the last century.

In fact, the tourist facilities are on a par with anywhere else in France. True, geography and demography determine the emphasis on rural simplicity. If sophisticated distractions are more modest than they are on the Côte d'Azur, so are the prices. Small, family-run hotels, each with its own character and idiosyncracy, are what the traveller outside the few big towns discovers. Confirmation of this is found in the annually revised *Guide des Hôtels Logis de France.* The *Logis*, which form the largest chain of hotels in the world, are mostly one- and two-star hotels where prices must always be inclusive. They, with the more modest *Auberges Rurales,* are well represented in the four *départements*; Puy-de-Dôme is most densely populated with them, followed by Cantal, Haute-Loire and Allier. Modest reliability might be the phrase best suited to describe the majority.

Some of the *Logis* hotels are in small villages, especially in the highlands of Puy-de-Dome, Cantal and Haute-Loire, which transform themselves for a few summer months into tiny, unpretentious resorts, where the air, the walks, the flowers, the scenery and modest hotel comforts create an atmosphere of tranquil revitalisation. Antignac, Saignes, Pailherols or Védrines-Saint-Loup spring to mind; many of them have pleasing architecture and unusual old rural churches as well.

Another chain of hotels is well represented in Auvergne. This is *France Accueil,* of whose 100 hotels nearly thirty are in the province, and some belong also to the *Logis de France.* They undertake to provide regional dishes, and give

Murat (Cantal)

advice and reading matter relating to local excursions. Out of season, one *France Accueil* hotel will book accommodation at another by telephone. In the high season, between July 1st and August 31st, the holiday can be booked ahead through the organisation's office in Clermont-Ferrand; this is a convenient arrangement allowing the use of interchangeable vouchers at *France Accueil* hotels, and packed lunches.

Similar arrangements can be made by the *Mapotel* chain whose hotels are rather more highly priced, for they are four-, three- and two-star establishments.

Few regular travellers in France are without their *Guide Michelin;* it is a miracle of annually correctly compressed information about hotels and restaurants. The gastronome looks out for tables which have been awarded rosettes for excellence. Only Hôtel de Paris in Moulins is given two rosettes in all Auvergne in the current guide. A dozen other places are thought to offer 'good food in its class', and merit one rosette.

Pitting one's palate against Michelin's judgement is a recognised and enjoyable game, provided one is not over-concerned with expense. I confess I have had more disappointing meals in rosetted restaurants than I have memorably enjoyed good ones. On the other hand, Michelin is almost invariably sound in recommending restaurants which give good food at moderate prices — marked with a red R in the guide. In this context, Auvergne fares well. More than twenty such establishments are listed, and I would always make for one of them.

The haul of luxurious hotels is small. There is Château St. Jean outside Montluçon, once belonging to the Knights Templars. There is Château de Codignat at Bort-l'Etang near Lezoux, a converted 15th century château, with its own heated swimming pool. Or else there is the Relais de Campagne of la Beaugravières at St. Germain-Lembron which specialises in such delicacies as *mousseline de foie de volailles* and *saumon source Choron.*

What else does Auvergne offer? Camp and caravan sites, of course, youth hostels, and self-catering *Gîtes ruraux*, furnished lodgings which must abide by certain minimum standards, are plentiful in village houses or farmhouses. On main roads are the familiar red and blue panels signalling the presence of *Relais routiers*, the French lorry-drivers' pull-ins. At many, substantial and relatively low-priced meals are served; at some a night's lodging can be obtained. The ambience is not invariably enticing.

*   *   *   •

As I indicated at the beginning of this chapter, disparagement of Auvergne's hotels and food still lingers. I would like to put the matter in perspective by outlining the diversity of food the province produces.

In the past, the gastronome has only conceded the greatness of Auvergnat cheese, plus, for a brief period in the 18th century, its frogs. They were imported to Paris by one Simon to create a fashion and make Simon's fortune. A century later, Alexandre Dumas said that frogs made a healthy diet, particularly in soup *'which helps some ladies to retain the freshness of their complexions'*.

Agricultural produce in the uplands may be limited, but lowland Auvergne has abundance. Quick transport and refrigeration bring convenience foods to the remoter parts, and traditional peasant diet of pork, potatoes and cabbage has become less obligatory. These ingredients still appear in dishes to which variety and ingenuity have been added. As everywhere else, there is a discrepancy between home and restaurant cooking. The traveller in Auvergne is most likely to judge its fare by what is served in restaurants; the smaller the restaurant the better the chance of individual attention to the cooking process. Temples of gastronomy — Michelin-style — cannot be expected in a pastoral province whose orientation towards an 'international palate' is, happily, localised and rudimentary.

*   *   *

A Cantal Farm

Crater Lake, Puy-de-Dôme

Cattle are mainly milch cows, but there is veal. Ample mutton produces regional dishes such as *gigot brayaude*, and stuffed sheep's trotters encased in tripe *(tripoux)* — less a regional delicacy than a bold venture into a substantial unknown, as someone has said. Chickens are plentiful; the Bourbonnais ones make a very good *coq au vin*.

Pig is the basis of the wide range of Auvergnat charcuteries: home-cured mountain ham *(jambon cru)*; sausages; stuffed pig's trotters *(pied de porc farci)*; pork pâté in a casing *(fricandeau)*; black pudding *(boudin)* with Cantal chestnuts; ham fillets with peppercorns. Pork and veal make the *tourte à la viande*. Fish is abundant.

Best known of Auvergnat dishes are the *potées*, or peasant stews of meat and vegetables cooked in a covered dish; indeed, they can be seen as very substantial soups in which pork, cabbage and potatoes form the major ingredients. A cabbage soup sounds simple, but recipes differ from place to place. It might be turnips, lard, pork, chicken and beef here, and salt pork, bacon, sausages, cabbage and beans there. Potatoes and cabbage form the base of *oeufs à l'Auvergnate*, when poached eggs are added.

These are some of the dishes prepared in the home; sometimes they appear as regional specialities on tourist menus in restaurants, and tourism has certainly encouraged local specialities which might otherwise have tended to die out.

There is quite a substantial list of them, such as the *friand sanflorain* from St. Flour, pork sausage meat with herbs in puff pastry or else wrapped in leaves — a refined kind of sausage roll. Lezoux and Clermont-Ferrand have their own hams; sometimes they are cooked in Madeira or *marc*. Sliced ham is the ingredient of recipes for omelettes, casserole chicken, or chicken *à la king*.

Le Puy is famous for its tiny green-brown lentils which so often accompany salt pork. Petits pois are the speciality of the Planèzes plateau of Cantal. Potato pie and cheese make up *truffado* of Aurillac; potatoes and cheese form the basis of various dishes known generically as *aligot*. When the dish is flavoured with garlic it is a speciality of Chaudes-Aigues. Also from Aurillac are sweet buckwheat pancakes or *bourriolles*. Montluçon produces a light, creamy potato purée. Brioude is noted for its thrushes *(grives)*.

Copper pots and pans are the traditional utensils of the French cuisine, nowhere more than in Auvergne. Antique and gift shops display them everywhere, and they shine on the walls of the more self-conscious restaurants. Not that there is always much resemblance between what is made today and what was in vogue earlier this century. Nowadays, copper strips are laminated in factories; few coppersmiths are left to fashion utensils in the traditional way, save perhaps in Aurillac. Here, they still make things with the irregular thickness handbeaten copper betrays; their bottoms are more substantial, and the joints are brazed. In the old days, copper utensils were cleaned with a polishing paste of rottenstone and whiting and then left in the sun to burnish.

After this little digression, mention should be made of desserts for these can be as substantial as main dishes. Pastries, pancakes, fruit flans and *clafoutis* or *milliard* — fruit, cherries in particular, baked whole in batter. *Brioches* (originally a pastry made with Brie cheese, and now a sweetish, soft, yellow bun-like bread eaten at breakfast) are a pride of Yssingeaux; a close relation is the *fouasse* from Cantal. Murat specialises in cream horns, *cornets de Murat*, and Vic-sur-Cère makes cream tarts, *tarte à la créme*. Mauriac produces its own kind of biscuit called *croquant*.

Candied fruits are a distinctive Auvergnat delicacy, made from the fruit of the Limagne. Sweets and chocolates abound, beautifully packaged and very expensive. If Vichy's confections of *pastilles* and *sucres d'orges* receive most publicity, Royat chocolates, Salers *carrées*, Néris-les-Bains *pastilles*, Aigueperse *pralines* almonds and *massepain* or marzipan, Bourbon-l'Archambault *truffettes* all demonstrate that the British are not alone in having a sweet tooth.

*   *   *

Now to Auvergne's cheeses. Most widely sold throughout France is Cantal cheese, with the longest history of unbroken production of any in France. Pliny the Elder wrote about it 2,000 years ago. When the Romans overran the coun-

Fromagerie at Bessé-en-Chandesse

try of the Arverni, a cheese industry already existed, for the natives made a huge breakfast meal of cheese, and the Romans, too, ate cheese for breakfast. Cantal then, was more or less as it is now. So, according to the historian of gastronomy and restauranteur, Raymond Oliver, a ewe-milk cheese was being made then similar to today's *Bleu d'Auvergne*, as was the *fourme d'Ambert*.

In times gone by, they produced their cheeses with traditional implements with delightful names such as *guerlou, freignale* or *atrassadou*. Local ethnic museums still show them. One such worth visiting is the *Musée de la Fourme paysanne* in the hamlet of Le Grand-Genévrier, eleven km north-northwest of Ambert, and housed in an old peasant storage building, the Jasserie du Coq Noir. Here the visitor can taste the *fourme* cheese and *brezou* — a bowl of milk straight from the cow, with rye bread. This little museum is open between 1st June and 30th September.

Back to Cantal cheese. At its best between November and May, Cantal is yellowish, crumbly, something between a Lancashire and Cheshire cheese. It is made either from the milk of the chestnut Salers or the Ferrandaise cows during summer. It is put into cylindrical moulds or *fourmes* (from the latin, *formas casei*, which also gave birth to the word *fromage*), and left to mature in the small stone huts that dot the Cantalian highland pastures and known as *burons* (or *jas* in the Forez). Shepherds spend (or used to spend) the summer here with their cattle which are enclosed overnight in stockades or *fumades*.

Variants of the classical *fourme* (or *fermier*) of Cantal appear in the smaller *Cantalon*, while the town of Laguiole makes its own version. Blue-veined varieties, such as *fourme d'Ambert* and *fourme de Montbrison* begin to resemble the great Roquefort of Aveyron, just to the south of our region.

In the cheese markets you will come across other Auvergnat cheeses. Well known in Britain is *Bleu d'Auvergne*, a Roquefort-like cheese of cow, goat and ewe milk. When mature between November and May, it is full and rich and sharp, and is sold in its silver paper with a green stripe. Variants are *Bleu de Salers, du Velay, de Thiezac,* and *Bleu de Laqueuille* which was the original *Bleu* of about a century ago and made of cows' milk only.

The tall, cylindrical cheeses with hard, marbled exteriors and blue veins inside, are the *fourmes d'Ambert*, a strong milk cheese. A smaller cheese from the same area is *Chevrotin d'Ambert*, a strong goat, or goat and milk, cheese. *Chevrotin de Moulins* is not dissimilar; this is sometimes sold under the generic name of *Chevrotin de Combrailles* (south of Montluçon), or *Bourbonnais*. Then there is the *Gaperon*, small, hard and spherical, made with cows' milk and flavoured with garlic. A thin round cheese of cow and goat milk is known as *La Rigotte*, changing its name to *La Brique* when square.

St. Nectaire is another outstanding cheese and comes from the Monts Dore. Soft, round, with a crust of yellowish-red, it is made from the milk of Salers and Ferrandaise cattle, maturing on straw mats in damp cellars where the conditions bring about the striking colour of the crust. *Vachard* and *Murol* (which has a hole in the middle) are related cheeses, at their best from October to July. A goat cheese from the vicinity of Aurillac and Salers is the *cabecou*.

*   *   *

'Official' wine maps of France leave Auvergne blank. The traveller would be forgiven for imagining that the province makes no wine. It does, of course.

Cheese-making in Auvergne

Not in the highlands, but modest *vins de pays* from the valleys are the little wines that are somewhat expensive on account of their limited production, but they are always worth trying.

When Caesar conquered Auvergne, there was no vine-growing and no wine-drinking, for all that the Arverni were highly advanced in the civilised arts and were wealthy. By the 5th century A.D., however, Sidonius (whom we shall meet again in a later chapter) was writing to a friend living near Clermont-Ferrand about his rich vineyards. He described Auvergne as possessing vineyards that clothed the slopes, and which were not irreparably destroyed by the barbarian invasions that coincided with the end of the Roman Empire in the west.

One of the first vineyards to be cultivated by the settling Romans was that of St. Pourçain-sur-Sioule in the Limagne. They must be among the oldest in France. White, red and rosé VDQS wines are produced, and they are the staple wines offered by restaurants in much of Auvergne. The white is pale and dry and the red softer and rounder; all three are very pleasant wines and can be tasted at the Maison du St. Pourçain.

Light red wines come from the Côte d'Auvergne, in the Clermont-Ferrand region. The best is Chanturgue, though not much is produced. A rarer red and rosé is Corent. Châteaugay appears on the wine lists of a number of restaurants, and is a red, while Veyre-Monton is a rosé. Some Beaujolais- like wines come from the Gamay vineyards of Coteaux du Forez near Montbrison (actually in the Loire *département*), and Brioude (where it is called Ribeyre), wines an older generation of connoisseurs looked down their noses at, but which are now being more highly esteemed. Apart from anything else, they are cheaper than Beaujolais.

Liqueurs of Auvergne have a wider reputation than the wines. Pre-eminent is the splendid cordial, Verveine du Velay and its close relative, Verveine du Puy. A wild verbena flavour dominates some thirty-two other herbs; the formula is, of course, secret. All liqueurs seem of necessity to be shrouded in alchemical secrecy to enhance their flavours. Verveine du Velay comes as a sweet and mild yellow cordial, and as a green and powerful one which, if swallowed carelessly, turns the Adam's apple area into a momentary Macbethian cauldron.

A much advertised aperitif is a gentian drink called commercially Arvèze; other Auvergnat liqueurs are flavoured with raspberry, strawberry (the best fresh strawberries come from Courpierre), myrtle and others I have never tried. One which I have goes by the name of Liqueur des Camisards, said to have been drunk by the Protestants who revolted in the Cévennes in the 18th century. I do not think it really helped their cause.

To end the chapter non-alcoholically, it may be noted that the various mineral waters of Auvergne are not necessarily used solely for medicinal purposes, but serve also to dilute wine. Most celebrated are Vichy's Célestins and Boussange which are faintly sparkling; Vichy St. Yorre which is salty and sparkling and a little unstable in its mineral contents; and Volvic, flat and full of volcanic trace elements.

Buttermilk or *gaspo*, it is said, is a favourite non-alcoholic drink in the region, but I dare say the tourist will experience a little difficulty in finding it.

5

IN DEFENCE OF SPAS

I must take care. In speaking up for the spas of Auvergne I cannot justify them from the medical standpoint which I do not have. I am merely an observer, aware of the shortcomings in medical practice and philosophy, and that the French, like ourselves, are avid consumers — and wasters — of pills and nostrums.

To many Frenchmen it might seem strange for a book to contain a justification of spas, which they accept as a natural adjunct to medicine. There are the spas, all over the place, whose abundance is to be accepted and fully made use of. True, younger French doctors sometimes share British scepticism about the value of spas, for the British have lost faith in their few spas and scoff at this 'taking of the waters'. However that may be, the hard facts are that about 1,200 springs in France are regarded as possessing medicinal properties. Administratively, spa therapy is incorporated into the French social security system, their equivalent to our National Health Service. Medical fees and the cost of treatment are covered by sickness insurance. In some cases, benefits include a person accompanying a patient to the spa. The word used to describe spa treatment is *thermalisme*, although not all waters are thermal.

Although *thermalisme* began in pre-Roman times, there have been long periods during which the therapeutic value was forgotten. Most French spas have a similar history. Pre-Roman Gaulish tribes venerated water, and they had their river and spring deities to whom temples were erected and offerings cast into the waters. When the Romans came, they were tolerant of native gods and modes of worship, even encouraging them if a local god bore some resemblance to a Roman one.

Part of religious worship was ritual immersion into pools whose healing properties were associated with the powers ascribed to gods or spirits of the place. No doubt specific therapeutic capabilities were recognised by special mineral contents, particularly at those springs where the water was hot and produced encrusting salts. Spiritual purification and the healing of ills were as close a unity for ancient Gauls as they were to be later for Christians prior to the dichotomy between spirit and matter constructed by the scientific outlook.

42

The Gauls held pilgrimages for those seeking relief for some afflication. The sufferer would present to the healing deity a little model, perhaps in wood or clay, of the afflicted part of the body. Such a healing spring was the one at Chamalières, known as Les Roches, near Clermont-Ferrand, which was active until the beginning of this century. Here, in 1968, were unearthed some 2,000 wooden votive images spread around the orifices of the now dried-up springs. They consisted of *'full figures, sometimes dressed in travellers' cloaks, heads, busts, arms and legs, animals and internal organs'* (Barry Cunliffe, *Rome and the Barbarians*). Some of the votives suggest that the spring's waters may have been used for the healing of eye complaints. The place had been used — though no temple was erected — by pilgrims and sick people for no more than about a century, until the middle of the 1st century A.D., to judge by the coins found among the votive offerings. Some of the latter were carvings of artistic worth, especially some of the cloaked travellers, and one of a figure with arms crossed over the chest, below which seems to be a carved impression of gastric organs. They were the forerunners of the carved ex-votos used at places of pilgrimage even today.

Wealthy Romans visited the fashionable spas of Royat (already used by the Arverni Gauls whose capital, Gergovia, was nearby), Vichy (*Aquae calidae*, hot waters), La Bourboule, Chaudes-Aigues, Evaux, Néris (*Neriomagus* in honour of the Gaulish god Nerios, and called *Aquae Nerii* by the Romans), and Bourbon-l'Archambault (also of Gaulish origin, as Borvo was the Gaulish Apollo). All are active spas today, and at most remains of Roman baths and other buildings have been revealed. Archaeologically, Néris is the most important. *Aquae Nerii* must have covered about 500 acres, and baths, aqueducts, temples, villas and an amphitheatre are moderately intact. With the exception of Les Roches at Chamalières, most medicinal springs, both in Auvergne and elsewhere in France, continued to flourish as long as the Roman Empire flourished in both its pagan and Christian phases. In a brief period of about fifty years, the Empire declined and fell in 420 A.D. Various tribes from Germany overran Gaul, and with them the medical and spiritual concept of healing waters evaporated. Only within the last two centuries have the curative properties been rediscovered.

Nowadays, around half a million people annually take spa cures in France. (Try getting a room in Bourbon-l'Archambault, even in September!) They have a curious atmosphere. Hospital and holiday resort blend; on the one hand is the sight of distressed sufferers moving painfully about the streets, and on the other are gay and bustling shops and cheerful folk out to enjoy themselves while taking the cure.

There is no shortage of cynics who speak of the gullible being milked at places where the only therapeutic result is through autosuggestion. Well, if the results with allopathic medicine were all that brilliant, one might lend an ear to the cynics. I think particularly of sufferers from unspectacular, chronic conditions, who, having failed to respond to drugs or anti-biotics, form a hard core with recourse to the slow methods of hydrotherapy. The medical specialists at the spas make only cautious claims, and they are careful to point out those conditions which are contra-indicated. It is the enthusiasm of the patients for their treatment that constitutes the real testimony.

Certainly, our cynics are quick to say that there are spas where the overfed and apparently unenlightened hedonists go for a ritual annual decoking before returning to the fleshpots of over indulgence. True, but that is a medical condition, nonetheless, and dieting at spas is also a prominent technique. And at all of them, more serious ailments are also dealt with.

Gone now are the old class structures which Europe's most distinguished spas once reflected — not least Vichy. Men and women in the public eye used to go there as much for social distraction as for the cure itself. They created fashion. A spa society centred on them. Madame de Sévigné visited Vichy to have her rheumatism treated in 1676 and 1677; she wrote with gushing enthusiasm to her daughter, doing a superb public relations job for the establishment. Vichy was graced by the daughter of Louis XV, by Napoleon's mother, and by the Emperor himself, taking a little time off from making war. He had the Vieux Parc laid out there in 1810. From 1861 on Napoleon III took the cure at Vichy and the *haute monde* followed him. The great and indestructible Talleyrand spent each August for thirty years at Bourbon-l'Archambault, holding audiences, conducting diplomatic moves, arranging parties.

Literary stars exerted a similar influence. Châtel-Guyon was patronised by Guy de Maupassant between 1866 and 1883. Royat drew the brothers Goncourt in 1867; Théophile Gautier, the romantic poet and novelist in 1869; Anatole France in 1875; as well as Maurice Barrès. Balzac incorporated Le Mont-Dore into a fanciful novel, *La Peau de Chagrin* (1831). George Sand had stayed at the resort in 1827 and used the experience in her novel *Jean de la Roche* (1860). Ana-

Le Mont Dore

tole France also spent a season at Le Mont-Dore and referred to it in *Jocaste* (1879) — without actually mentioning the shabby little place by name. A galaxy of illustrious names secured an intellectual respectability for the spas of Auvergne. Would a Samuel Beckett or a Jean-Paul Sartre aid a fresh influx today? It might have to be a Burton, Beatle or Bardot.

The thermo-mineral springs of Auvergne tend to concentrate either along the geological fault lines, especially along each side of the Limagne valley which had subsided, or else within the volcanic areas. Vichy and Châteldon, for instance, are on the eastern side; Châtel-Guyon and Royat are on the western side of the Limagne. La Bourboule, Le Mont-Dore and St. Nectaire lie in the centre of the volcanic mass.

*   *   *

Volcanic soils are immensely rich in minerals, with carbonic acid predominating; each spa has differing mineral compositions whose therapeutic properties are indicated for a wide variety of ailments. In their passage underground along channels and fissures, rainwater and subterranean streams or condensed volcanic gases that have been submitted to high pressure, act on the chemicals suspended in the rocks. Chemical salts are absorbed into the water whose heat is acquired from underground pressures; the deeper the subterranean water course, the hotter is the resurgent water. At the surface, each spring retains a constant temperature, although not always a constant supply, as is the case with the Bellerive source near Vichy. An intermittent source, its flow is regulated by rising temperatures below which expand gases enough to push water to the surface. Then follows a period of contraction when no water reaches the surface until some eight hours later. The cycle of expansion and contraction is repeated.

An indication of the thinness of Auvergne's rock crust, created initially by the thrusts of the continental drift, is that for every thirteen metres, the heat of the rock rises one degree centigrade. This is a much more rapid temperature increase than with non-volcanic rocks.

*   *   *

This is not a medical treatise. I shall do no more than mention the work done at a few of the better known spa-centres, beginning with La Bourboule. It deserves to be more widely known in Britain because it treats those all too familiar conditions of asthma and bronchitis. La Bourboule, at 852m, lies in the wide and pretty valley of the Dordogne, and its site was once a lake. The bulk of patients are children. Medicinally, the waters are drunk, used in baths, douches, sprays and inhalation (*pulvérisation*). Like most other resorts, La Bourboule is open from spring until autumn, and courses of treatment, under medical supervision, last in the region of three weeks. La Bourboule announces itself as the 'capital of allergy'. Its waters contain more arsenic than do any-

La Bourboule — Spa resort

others in France. It sounds lethal, but it is the basis of the spa's treatment of pathological conditions. Also, the waters are highly radioactive and rich in rare gases such as helium, neon, argon, crypton and xenon.

Respiratory allergies are the conditions most frequently treated, but anaemia and eczema also respond to the arsenical waters. French doctors have frequently said that severe and widespread bronchial disabilities are not the medical worry they would be but for the existence of La Bourboule.

Somewhat similar conditions are treated at nearby Le Mont-Dore, rather higher and cooler than La Bourboule, with the difference that the ratio of adults to children is roughly the reverse of what it is at La Bourboule. Le Mont-Dore has also established itself as a winter sports' centre.

Vichy styles itself 'queen of watering places'. Its rapid expansion as a modern leisure resort has already been described. What has changed less is the treatment; perhaps for those with liver complaints who drink the waters in the Grande Grille, the ritual is much as it used to be, even if less grand than in yesteryears. But there is more to Vichy's treatment than drinking not entirely palatable water.

Vichy has almost two hundred springs whose mineral contents and temperatures vary a little, and which all contain sodium bicarbonate — a familiar ingredient but in a different suspension — potassium bicarbonate, calcium and magnesium, chloride and sulphate, some arsenic — Vichy, the 'queen of arsenic', is the jibe of hostile critics — phosphates, and trace elements. Taken internally, the waters are said by Vichy medical pundits to have no peer in the treatment of hepatic and digestive ailments. They deal with migraine and diabetes as well. Children with disordered livers respond most favourably of all. Applied externally, the water stimulates circulation and deals with certain skin disorders. Exported Vichy waters come from the Célestins cold spring.

All the complex conditions associated with gastro-intestinal malfunction are the province of Châtel-Guyon. For the most part, patients drink water rich in magnesium chlorate; they take baths and vegetal-mineral mud packs in one of Europe's most up-to-date hydrotherapeutic centres.

Chaudes-Aigues in Cantal is unusual. So hot are its natural waters at 82° C that they are put to various domestic uses, such as the town's hot water supply and central heating. Which is what the Romans did at Chaudes-Aigues 2,000 years ago. Some of the town's water pipes are made of pine wood. The almost boiling sodium bicarbonate, radioactive and stimulating water is used chiefly to treat muscular rheumatism, gout, sciatica, neuralgia and old wounds. Rheumatism is also the specialisation of Châteauneuf-les-Bains.

Vichy, 'Queen of Watering Places'

In the northern part of our region, Néris-les-Bains lies on the fringe of the Massif Central. It has had a longer history of unbroken thermal medicine than most spas. Its insipid-tasting water feels slightly oily to the touch, probably due to the vegetable matter in the water which is used to treat disorders of the nervous system. The guide book says the calming and sedative properties are successful with cases of hysteria, neurasthenia, locomotor ataxia, and all the neuroses — an interesting approach to a field normally left to the psychiatrist. Secondary indications are female disorders (note the implication of the classical association between female disorders and hysteria), and skin trouble deriving from arthritis, and neuro-arthritic disorders in children.

Untypically, Bourbon-l'Archambault is open all the year round to receive rheumatic patients. Royat, almost a suburb of Clermont-Ferrand, also has a longer season than most, being open between April and mid-November. It was revived early in the 19th century as a spa for heart disorders after centuries of oblivion.

Near the Puy de Sancy in the Monts Dore is St. Nectaire surrounded by pine forests. The town straggles out into two parts along the narrow valley of the Courançon; the lower one is where the thermal establishment is, and deals with kidney complaints. The upper one is a cheerful little holiday village which we shall meet again later, for it contains an outstanding example of 12th century Auvergnat architectural art.

In addition to these hydromineral centres — and I have by no means mentioned them all — are climatic stations where atmospheric pressure, warmth, light, purity of air, or some other factors are regarded as having particular medical value. All these places in Auvergne lie in Cantal: Le Lioran-Laveissiere at 1,150m; St. Flour at 783m, and Vic-sur-Cère at 700m. The latter is also a spa whose cold and pleasantly tasting waters help to treat gastritis, liver and kidney troubles, anaemia and malarial recurrences. Specialists will no doubt be able to explain how the same waters can cope successfully with such an assortment of seemingly unrelated pathologies.

Some readers may be taken aback at a chapter on morbidity in a travel book. This is not as incongruous as it may at first seem. French doctors who specialise in *thermalisme* recognise the need to unite treatment with leisure, so that the latter becomes a stimulus, a therapeutic agent to the former. Phrases like environmental medicine, psychosomatic medicine, or ecological medicine are rather cumbersome ways of expressing what people like Madame de Sévigné and, who knows? the old Arverni tribes of Gaulish Auvergne were doing quite spontaneously.

It is time, anyway, that we met them in the next chapter.

6

FROM THE CELTS TO TODAY

Once again, when dealing with the far-distant past, we must speak of the Massif Central as a whole, a natural geographical entity; any semblance of Auvergne's territorial reality comes only late in historical times.

The Massif Central's pre-history is nothing like as stimulating as that of its neighbours. There is no magnificent Palaeolithic cave art as in Périgord; no pre-Roman Hellenistic and Iberian influences as are still visible in Languedoc and Provence. The great communicating corridor of the Rhône valley, itself rich in antiquity, leads into the Rhône-Saône corridor, and gave Burgundy the sumptuous Hallstattian hill-fort and burial site of Vix whose wonderful bronze *krater* from a Corinthian workshop has been dated to 575 B.C. The land structure of the Massif Central explains the relative poverty of prehistoric finds.

In the Upper Palaeolithic period which lasted from 33,000 B.C. to 10,000 B.C., France, outside the Mediterranean belt, was subjected to glaciation, save in the warm, sheltered valleys as in Périgord where the first peak of true human culture occurred — the Magdalenian cave art. Early Magdalenian man did not venture into the higher valleys of the Massif Central, but his successors did. They developed new techniques with which to make barbed weapons out of reindeer antlers — sometimes engraved — and novel types of flint tools with which to hunt, fish and gather food, and venture into the Massif from Périgord, the Rhône valley and Burgundy. They followed the Loire and the Allier, the Jordanne, Corrèze and Sourdoire; they crossed the Limousin plateau, using whatever cave shelter there was.

In the Neolithic, between 4,000 B.C. and 1,800 B.C., lowland life was being transformed through the domestication of sheep, later of cattle and pigs; new ways of making pottery were evolved; they discovered stone polishing, textile weaving and metallurgy with copper, gold and silver — a technological revolution originating in the Mediterranean. It came only slowly to the Massif Central. To its south, Neolithic pastoralism was associated with limestone plateaux which in those days were more wooded and humid than now. There is an almost sudden barrier between the limestone Neolithic megalithic tombs

49

and the non-limestone formations in the Massif, for Aveyron, abutting onto Cantal, has more such tombs than any other *département* in France. Settlers who may have come from Almeria in Spain, landing on the Languedoc coast at Frontignan, prospected for copper in the 2nd century B.C. They were builders, pastoralists and seasonal nomads who spread north, erecting for the privileged ranks of their society chamber tombs. Those in Aveyron are already simpler than those nearer the coast. Auvergne has few such monuments. There are some on the *planèze* of St. Flour. Best known is the large one at St. Nectaire, and is the most northerly relic of a Neolithic community to have explored beyond the Causses of Languedoc, following reindeer as the climate became less severe.

The megaliths of cultures penetrating the Massif from the north are seen in the valleys of the Allier and Dordogne, and on the Monts de Blond, a little granite outpost of the western Massif Central. Drystone huts were erected on the Auvergnat plateaux.

During the Bronze Age (1,800 B.C. - 600 B.C.) various factories making arms and ornaments were set up in the Massif, and there was considerable long-distance trading. For example, swords, spearheads and torcs, manufactured in England and Ireland, were bought in Auvergne. With the appearance of the Urnfield culture from Germany, by which the dead were cremated in urns and buried in flat graves, weapons, pottery and ornaments were laid in the graves.

Cantal Pastures

They have been unearthed in various parts of Auvergne, particularly at Dompierre-sur-Besbre (Allier).

While the Urnfield culture declined elsewhere in Gaul by the end of the 8th century B.C., it lingered in the Massif until the 2nd century B.C.

As a result of far-away disturbances in Eastern Europe and the Aegean, people known as Proto-Celts moved into Western Europe about 1,500 B.C. They entered Gaul in waves from Southern Germany and Alsace, and gradually evolved a distinctive art and tradition of very high quality, as well as the Celtic culture which contained elements of ethnic unity. The Greeks knew them as *Keltoi*; the Romans as *Galli*; later both Greeks and Romans used the term *Galatae*. The Celts made iron instruments to open up new areas for agriculture and forest felling; they made the iron slashing sword for use in war. Of this iron age there seem to be few signs in the Massif. They developed trade, barter and coinage; one trade route lay across the Cévennes so as to deal with the merchants of Marseille.

The Celtic Biturges tribe occupied the territory between Loire, Allier and Vienne, with *Avaricum* (Bourges) as their capital. The Arverni occupied the plains of the Allier and the mountains southwards, with their capital at *Gergovia*, today's Gergovie outside Clermont-Ferrand. From the Saône to the plateau of Autun and the Loire were lodged the Aedui. The Velavi were ensconced in the Velay hills, while the Gabali and Ruteni flanked the Arverni in the south, in Gévaudan and Rouergue respectively. In Quercy lived the Cadurci.

At first, the Biturges were the dominant tribe under their legendary chief, Ambigat. By the 2nd century B.C. the Arverni endeavoured to weld some kind of empire between the Atlantic and the Rhine. Their kings lived in sumptuous splendour, and Luern drove out in a silver-plated chariot to scatter gold among his people. His son, Bituitus, was captured by the Romans and died in Rome in 121 B.C. With the exception of the Aedui, all the tribes formed a fragile coalition under the leadership of the Arvernian chief, Vercingétorix, at the time of the Roman conquest of 52 B.C.

In more ways than the Romans would have cared to admit, the Celts were their superiors in technology such as mining, metallurgy, farming and stock-raising. Their fatal flaw was in organisation and discipline. The volatile Celts of the Massif Central were loyal to local chiefs; militarily, they were beaten before they fought. Moreover, they had no written language. All knowledge and tradition had to be handed on by word of mouth and retained in well-trained memories. Until the 5th century A.D. they were illiterates who responded to the explosive passions of rhetoric. The best orator, the most eloquent leader, the most arresting hyperbolist, gained the people's allegiance. The intellectual, philosophical, religious and scientific attainments in this heroic, vivacious, headstrong, quarrelsome and undisciplined society were considerable.

Arvernian Vercingetorix, son of Celtillus who *'had held suzerainty over all Gaul, and had been put to death by his compatriots for seeking to make himself king'* (Caesar, *The Conquest of Gaul*), led an uprising against the Romans in the winter of 53 - 52 B.C. He concentrated his forces on the hill of Gergovia, the Arvernian capital, and temporarily checked Caesar — thereby sowing the seeds of a legend about a great victory — before being defeated at Alésia in Burgundy, imprisoned for five years, and then put to death.

Today's Gergovic is a bleak plateau; in 1862 it still went by the unappetising name of Merdogne, when Napoleon III had the site excavated to reveal Caesar's camp below the plateau. Later digs extended the findings and confirmed, if confirmation were needed, Caesar's descriptive precision in his *Conquest of Gaul*. The Gallic hillfort or *oppidum* on the plateau has also been excavated.

After Caesar's victory and the subjugation of the whole of Gaul, life in the Massif Central continued much as before. The old kings of Gaul vanished to be replaced by magistrates. But the nobles remained powerful, and one, Epasnactus, who supported the Romans, issued his own coins. The peasants produced crops as rich as the land allowed; there were large landed proprietors and country villas; the vine was planted and the Limagne marshes drained; the skills of local craftsmen were extended. Roman building techniques were adopted, and the thermal spas were put on a sound commercial-medical basis. Metalwork, mining, enamel work, bronze statuettes or clay figurines of deities, carpentry, barrel-making (invented by the Gauls) — all these activities were pursued.

Pottery was perhaps the major industry in the Allier valley. A potter named Saturninus was associated with a group of Arvernian potters at Martres-de-Veyre near Clermont-Ferrand, and from about 80 A.D. introduced a new style which *'combined decorative features from central and southern Gaul and made abundant use of patterns of great finesse and delicacy copied or moulded from the dies used in the production of metal ornaments'* (J.J. Hatt, *Celts and Gallo-Romans*). Saturninus was also responsible for introducing mass-production.

Earlier, around 10 A.D., a school of pottery had been started at Lezoux. Here, the human figure was introduced. More workshops were set up in the vicinity to exploit the growing popularity of *terra sigillata*, the ware being covered with an impermeable slip of brilliant red. It was exported from Lezoux mainly by navigable waterways as far as Antioch and Britain. Lezoux is a nondescript town on the edge of the Limagne plain. 160 Gallo-Roman potters' kilns within a radius of three km have been discovered, and examples of Lezoux pottery are shown in its museum, including the so-called Mithra vase with appliqué reliefs of Mithras slaughtering the bull. This suggests that Gaulish myths and religious practices absorbed this Roman-imported Oriental cult, just as the Oriental mystery cults of Cybele and Attis had been absorbed. Another handsome discovery at Lezoux was a 1st century statue, now at St. Germain-en-Laye, of a solid, bearded, bourgeois-looking elderly Gaul, the

Gaulish god Esus (the Romans equated him with Mercury), here in his role as protector of trade, for he carries a money-bag in his right hand.

The main pre-historical and Gallo-Roman museums are in these towns: Aurillac, Clermont-Ferrand, Gergovie, Glozel, Lezoux, Moulins, Murol, Néris-les-Bains, Le Puy and St. Flour.

*   *   *

When, in 27 B.C., Augustus divided Gaul into four provinces, Auvergne became the possession of Aquitania. He imposed taxes on land and all property, and instituted the census. Old tribal units were retained, but the Arverni's capital was renamed *Augustonemetum* and brought down to the valley to where Clermont-Ferrand now lies. The Augustan system was to last for three centuries.

During this time seven evangelists came from Rome — in 250 A.D. — to convert Gaul to Christianity. St. Austremoine preached to the Arverni and became the first bishop of Clermont. His disciples founded the Auvergnat churches, with St. Nectaire at Champeix, St. Geneys at Thiers, St. Antoninus at Gannat, St. Mary at Brioude, and St. Florus in the St. Flour region.

The word 'isolation' recurs as the underlying theme to an understanding of Auvergne's history. Isolation left Auvergne in comparative peace and prosperity when the Alaman invasions under Crocus took place in 270 A.D., even though Clermont was sacked. Also, towards the end of the 5th century, as the Roman Empire in the west broke up, when the Visigoths invaded the region.

Demolition of the Roman Empire fell to the Frankish barbarian Clovis who had himself baptised as much out of political opportunism as through the devoutness of his wife. He acquired most of Gaul for himself, so that on his death in 511, the Kingdom of the Franks comprised all France save the southwest and south, the Lowlands and part of Germany. But such political boundaries on the map were in those days more notional than real. There were innumerable fiefdoms, most of them unruly and autonomous, and the kingdom was constantly redivided by quarrelling offspring of the king. What we call Auvergne was little more than a transit region.

By the early 8th century, Auvergne under its counts, was part of the dukedom of Aquitaine which became absorbed by the Carolingians. It was the powerful rule of Charles the Great — Charlemagne — who held the throne for forty-six years from 768 to 814 which forged an empire through vassalage of Franks and Lombards, reaching from beyond the Pyrenees to far into eastern Europe and included Italy as far south as Rome. After his death, the unwieldy Carolingian empire began to fall apart. It was divided between Charlemagne's grandsons, and Auvergne was acquired by the Kingdom of Charles to become a frontier province with the Kingdom of Lothar.

The 9th century saw the invasions of the Normans, and the towns of Clermont and Brioude were both burned and pillaged. Hungarians attacked Auvergne from the east, and Tunisian Saracens from their base in the Maures mountains of Provence, and Marseille. In consequence of the Norman drive southwards, many monks from the Atlantic part of France where the attacks were most severe, fled to Auvergne to found new monasteries, encouraging local agricultural production.

Feudalism in the 10th century meant lawlessness because no-one recognised the central authority of the king, and it meant an anarchical defence of independence by counts and their vassals. The best the king could hope to achieve was to remain on top of the feudal heap and devise methods for ensuring succession (primogeniture) and retaining some authority. One can see here the origins of the periodic French search for stronger centralised government. Auvergne became covered with castles in the most impregnable positions. Their owners fought one another; above all, they fought the crown. They also jockeyed for position by short-lived alliances and by marriages. The smaller manor of Bourbonnais, round Bourbon-l'Archambault, between the 10th and 13th centuries enlarged itself through royal favour, marriages and wills to encompass the Bourbonnais, Forez, the county of Marche, as well as the whole county, duchy and dauphiny of Auvergne. By the end of the 15th century, the House of Bourbon had established itself as the most powerful in the kingdom with its court at Moulins.

*   *   *

But to go back a little, the dukedom of Aquitaine which included Auvergne became the property of Richard I, Richard Coeur-de-Lion (1157 - 99) by gift of his father, Henry II, who had acquired it by marriage to Eleanor of Aquitaine. Richard was forced to abandon it to Philippe Auguste, Philippe II, the Capet king, in 1189. Philippe organised an expedition into Auvergne where he made Riom the administrative seat; the town's prosperity started from that time. By 1211 the Dukedom of Auvergne was reunited with the French crown, except Haute-Auvergne which was its own administrative dominion by the middle of the 13th century: the *Baillage des Montagnes*.

In spite of successive attacks upon it, Clermont (medieval *Clarus mons*) remained a large and important town. Here, in 1095, Pope Urbain II launched the First Crusade, an inspired and ambitious appeal for men to recover Jerusalem from the Muslims, and wear the sign of the Cross on their apparel. The crowds gathered about the papal throne cheered ecstatically, crying 'God

St. Nectaire

wills it!', and the enthusiasm spread throughout Europe. Religious life was vigorous in many parts of Auvergne between the 10th and 13th centuries, due in some measure to the influential proximity of the abbey of Cluny in Burgundy. This powerful Benedictine order had been founded in 910 by an Auvergnat, William of Aquitaine, and many of the abbots were also from Auvergne.

In 1337 the Hundred Years War began. The English kings claimed the throne of France while, concurrently, the feudal structure of France was beginning to break up through the efforts of the Capetian kings to centralise their political authority. The French refused to surrender sovereignty over territories in France; the English refused to give up their dynastic pretensions. Why should they? Huge customs revenues from the wine and wool trades were levied in Bordeaux for the benefit of the English throne. England supplied Bordeaux with wheat, salted fish, wool and cloth, for at the time of the War's outbreak, Edward III was still ruler of Gascony and Guienne.

Auvergne was part of the English possession. At first the war was fought in the north and Auvergne was little disturbed. Later, she was to feel the consequences — military, social and economic — of the devastations caused by that most hated of rulers of Aquitaine, Edward, the Black Prince, and by the Free Companies. These were the *routiers*, or disbanded mercenaries, who spread misery throughout the region. It experienced poverty, disease, excessive taxation. Towns declined as whole populations fled as refugees.

The Black Prince was exhausted by the military skill of Bertrand du Guesclin who also decimated the Free Companies. In his last campaign against the English, in 1380, du Guesclin planned to attack the castle of Carlat near Aurillac, but he died outside Châteauneuf-de-Randon (Lozère), while laying siege to the English garrison. There is a statue to him in the town. His entrails are in the church of St. Laurent in Le Puy; he was re-embalmed at Montferrand, and his remains were scattered by the revolutionaries in 1793.

Advantages won for the French by du Guesclin were thrown away in the reign of Charles VI (1380 - 1422). Charles VII hoped to regain his kingdom and organised some resistance to the English. His lack of success made him think of fleeing to the mountains of Auvergne. At that moment, the spirit of confidence among the half-hearted French troops was rekindled by Joan of Arc (1412 - 31). She passed through Moulins and sought the aid of Riom and Clermont in the elimination of English troops from French soil.

Joan of Arc, with no military abilities, was the embodiment of religious rebirth and consciousness of nationhood. For the first time can France be spoken of as a country in the modern sense.

Round Tower, Murol

Bourbon l'Archambault

Much first-hand information about a part of the Hundred Years War as it affected Auvergne, comes from the chronicler Jean Froissart (1337 - 1410). We have his description how the celebrated captain of a *Grande Compagnie*, Aymerigot Marchez (there are numerous spellings of the name) was captured at Dyke de la Roche-Vendeix, near La Bourboule in 1390. Or the wedding festivities at Riom in June 1389 of Jean, Duc de Berry, and Jeanne, daughter of Jean de Boulogne and Auvergne. Or how the innumerable (and mostly unenforceable) truces between the English and the French were arranged by commissioners. Froissart imparted to tragic and often sordid events an aura of chivalric heroism.

During the Middle Ages, the capital of the Dukedom of Auvergne was Riom. Under Charles VII, the Dukedom was given to the Bourbons, and Riom was regarded as joint capital with Clermont of Auvergne. Almost throughout its history, the province had been plagued by a tyrannical and turbulent nobil-

58

ity, always able to retreat to the security of the mountains. To put an end to this rebellious state of affairs, Louis XIV set up a commission in Clermont in 1665 to listen to complaints against injustices by the Auvergnat nobles. This was the period of the *Grands Jours d'Auvergne*, when a number of nobles were executed. The rest fled; they were executed in effigy, to the joy of the peasants. But the misery left behind taxed all the skills of able governors or *intendants*, who brought road building, drainage of marshlands, and agricultural revival.

In the middle of the 16th century the Wars of Religion gave rise to implacable hostilities between Catholics and Protestants. Auvergne, predominantly Catholic, suffered from the cruel and rapacious Protestant fanatic — we might call him a psychopath — Captain Merle (1548 - 90) who led a small band of men. In 1575 he captured Issoire and meted out fearful punishment. Two years later, the Catholic army of the Duke of Anjou laid siege to Issoire and sacked it. Another anti-Catholic fanatic, Baron des Adrets, rampaged far and wide, including the Forez hills. You were either for the King or for the League. Not until Henri IV (1553 - 1610), the first of the Bourbon dynasty, could peace be restored.

*   *   *

Provincial administration was dissolved with the French Revolution. What had been the Bourbonnais became the *département* of Allier; Auvergne became Puy-de-Dôme and Cantal; Velay, Haute-Loire. From then on, all *départements* were administered by prefects appointed by the central government in Paris. It is so today.

With the end of the Napoleonic wars and the end of Napoleon I, a shaky monarchy was restored in France. Had the republican Auvergnat, La Fayette been half-way competent he could have created another republic in 1830, such was the unpopularity of the monarchy and the heritage of Napoleon I.

Compared with other regions, Auvergne's prosperity fell away during the early 19th century, and only the coming of the railways in mid-century began to give the remote uplands the outlets they needed. Even though Clermont-Ferrand expanded its industrial capabilities through rubber, there remained an atmosphere of somnolence and decline which only the last thirty years have dissipated. For Auvergne, like the rest of France, never really had an industrial revolution as did England and Germany. If at all, it is now, and not a little credit for it must go to the Michelin Tyre Company in Clermont-Ferrand.

In the desperate and despairing years before and during the 1939 - 45 war, when decisions by western European politicians were stop-gap and bred of uncertainty, fame of a kind visited Auvergne.

Socio-political tensions between Left and Right were acute and found reflection in the then sternly paternalistic hostility of the Michelin directors in Cler-

Monument to the Maquis, *Mont Mouchet*

mont-Ferrand during the 1930s towards any militancy by the trades unions in the Michelin factories. There was the Hoare-Laval Pact of 1935 which ensured that Italy enjoyed a free hand in its conquest of Ethiopia. The Pact had been negotiated by Sir Samuel Hoare and the French foreign minister, Pierre Laval, the Auvergnat lawyer and politician. For ten unhappy years, Laval was at the centre of French political life.

After the French defeat in 1940, Vichy became the seat of the Pétain government, where Pierre Laval could exercise his skill at cunning intrigue to get the

Davayat, Puy de Dôme

best bargain possible out of the victorious Germans. Vichy housed a motley assortment of adventurers, fanatics, idealists, opportunists, a representative mixture of outlooks fashioned by years of indecision, failure, and sudden military disaster. These sad associations with the spa of Vichy were matched by the notorious trials at Riom in 1942 of men who were held responsible for the defeat of 1940 — Léon Blum, Paul Daladier, Paul Reynaud and General Gamelin.

Intense resistance to the German forces was organised in Auvergne, for the Massif Central was the region through which German reinforcements had to pass to support their troops combatting the Allied invasion. A major battle was fought on June 10th 1944 on Mont Mouchet, not far from St. Flour. The site has been adopted as the national monument to the *maquis*, where the foresters' house has been converted into a resistance museum, for here had been the headquarters of the French Forces of the Interior in Auvergne.

Since 1945, Auvergne has been launched into modernity, into industry, communications, the media, the supermarkets, tourism, and is evolving, for better in the short term and for worse in the longer, an urban mentality.

Only some of Auvergne is making the brash advance away from the disastrous stagnation of the inter-war years. Poverty and the hard life can still go hand in hand with the gleaming television set. Parts of the province still seem to be populated by the old men who have an eternal quality in France. Elsewhere, though, Auvergne, like the rest of France, is growing younger.

7

LIVELIHOOD, TRADITION AND CHANGE

Massive planning and modernisation schemes, new educational programmes, technological advances and subsidies have been applied throughout France, but Auvergne's first concern is with its agricultural development. The total number of farms in France is diminishing fast; there are now probably only half the number of 1955. In Auvergne, the decline is higher, due in part to joint farming projects (*Groupements agricoles d'exploitation commun*), partly through amalgamations as smaller and uneconomical farms become absorbed by larger units.

The Limagne valley — fertile and climatically mild — is densely populated with over eighty people to each square km; the uplands are sparsely populated, for there are few alternative jobs. Compared with the rest of France, Puy-de-Dôme and Haute-Loire have a fairly high percentage of population living on farms; in Cantal, the figure is low.

Throughout history, the black soil of the Limagne has created wealth. Wheat is still the most important crop, along with sugar beet, maize, sunflower, potatoes, vegetables and high quality seed production. Tobacco grows outside Riom. Vineyards — sometimes interspersed with fruit trees — line the plain's flanks. Above, grow apples and pears and strawberries. Higher still are peaches, apricots, cherries and almonds that supply local markets and confectionery factories. Cattle are raised, fattened for two or three years on large estates before being driven to local cattle markets or further afield to Poitou and Berry. Sheep destined for mutton, and poultry — at Jaligny-sur-Besbre a poultry market is held every Wednesday, and in mid-December Jaligny becomes the turkey capital of France — are less conspicuous sources of wealth.

Moulins, Varennes, Vichy, Thiers and Riom are all close to the Limagne. So is Clermont-Ferrand, now a major provincial town with a population exceeding 200,000, whose industries are dominated by Michelin which employs ten percent of the total population. The once marshy Limagne of Clermont has been drained and put to intensive agricultural use.

Moulins, a major regional market, also produces furniture and clothes.

Hides do not have far to travel to supply the tanneries and shoe factories. Furniture is also made at Varennes-sur-Allier; timberyards and sawmills dot the valley of the Dore. Riom, apart from its tobacco industry, makes electric cables and engineering tools, and has distilleries and brickworks. Its sawmills are not for cutting timber but the hard-grained blocks of Volvic lava.

Thiers is the French cutlery capital. If the visitor expects a Sheffield-in-Auvergne, he is due for a surprise. A handsome town, the buildings clinging to the steep hillsides above the river, look clean and brilliant as one approaches from the southern side with the afternoon light falling on the hundreds of façades. An old industry has kept abreast without destroying its environment. Thiers' cutlery industry has its origins in the Crusades, when the secret of tempering steel was brought back. Still largely an artisanal industry, it commands more than three-quarters of all French steel-cutting instrument production, and has diversified into jewellery, stainless steel, plastics, kitchen utensils, surgical instruments and motor-car accessories.

Elsewhere, old industries give way to new. Ambert, once world famous for its 300 mills manufacturing paper in the 14th to 17th centuries, makes a living out of plastics, braid, lace and rosaries (though hand-made lace is in steep decline, as at Le Puy). The relics of the paper industry are confined to an excellent museum at Moulin Richard-de-Bas. Vic-le-Comte is where water-marked paper is made, and the bank notes of France are printed at Chamalières.

That far-seeing 17th century statesman, Jean-Baptiste Colbert (1619 - 83) brought new life to decaying Aurillac with lace-making, gold- and silver-smithing, tanning, jewellery-making, and the forging of braziers for charcoal burning. They declined in turn, and now Aurillac is an important agricultural centre, makes furniture, cheap ironmongery and — aided by its climate — umbrellas and gumboots.

Specialist industries have sprung up in many small towns; pharmaceuticals at Vertolaye, and glass-works at St. Yorre, for bottling the waters of Vichy.

At the end of the 18th century, Montluçon in Allier was a large village. From 1830 it expanded through the exploitation of its iron ore deposits and coal seams. The coal was easily and cheaply transported when the Canal du Berry was dug. Early this century, the seams were exhausted. Great hardship hit the town until the introduction of aluminium, chemical, textile and tyre industries (Dunlop have a factory there). Commentry nearby has had a similar history. At Champagnac-les-Mines in Cantal, on the 'coal furrow', mining was abandoned in 1959 and a rich uranium deposit was discovered instead.

Most of these industries are of no great attraction to the visitor, but the

Thiers, Puy de Dôme

An Auvergnat Home

hydro-electric schemes, harnessing the numerous westward flowing rivers of Auvergne, are often handsome and impressive.

*   *   *

These illustrations indicate the thriving places. The poor regions, with few natural resources other than reforestation, depend more on tradition. To them, population decline is familiar. It is itself traditional. Unskilled workers sought a living in Paris. Mauriac used to send scrap-metal dealers to Rouen;

Auvergnat bed, Ambert

men from the Jordanne valley went to work at the Lyon furnaces; muleteers went from the Dore valley to the Rhône to sell their beasts; others went to Nantes to trade in sardines. In winter, men from many Cantalian towns would carry cloth over almost impassable roads to earn a few extra *sous*. Or they were tinkers or water-carriers. Condat-en-Féniers is still the Auvergnat centre for *colportage*; vans loaded with cloth and materials are driven round the countryside, and when their owners have made their pile, they return and build themselves comfortable country houses. Young men and women have

67

Lac Chambon

for long left home, unskilled, spending the whole of their working lives else-where; the successful ones returned to retirement, sometimes to the remotest corners of Auvergne. They are hard working, strong and resourceful, the Auvergnats.

Further back in history, from the Middle Ages to the 16th century, the pattern of life was simple. The kitchen was the centre of the home; its fire never went out. There was dearth in winter; the spring was for feasting, and the woman in the kitchen was the gastronomic alchemist of those times. Feudal Auvergne lived by the three basic principles of work, food and sex. When that sagacious philosopher Montaigne visited Auvergne in the 16th century, he observed that 'barbarism is to distance oneself from nature'.

In the 19th century, the Auvergnats were not so much undernourished as living on an unbalanced diet. Country people ate huge quantities of black bread — up to 400 kg a year for each adult — and only a little soup, lard, walnut oil, no meat, no wine. Hence the small men. They had undernourished cattle; the bulls had strength only for half a day's work. There were few horses. Cows produced milk only during lactation, and then about five litres a day; over a year that averaged a litre a day. Land was left fallow every other year. In the mountains, it was cultivated one year and lay fallow for five. The ploughs had to be about a fifth lighter than those in Languedoc.

68

Cantal drystone buron

Once thin crops of rye and buckwheat have given way to more pastureland. Upland arable is more extensive: wheat, winter wheat especially, barley, oats, potatoes, fodder crops, lentils.

Poor pastures — they cover a third of Puy-de-Dome and Haute-Loire and half of Cantal — are given over to stock-rearing. Cattle are stall-fed on fodder crops during the long winters, put into water-meadows in spring, and taken to high pastures in early summer until autumn. More than half are dairy cattle. In Cantal one sees the mahogany coloured Salers on the rain-soaked grasses on basalt rock above 800m. During the last century, Tyssandier d'Escous (1813 - 89) of Salers refined the breed whose milk produces Cantal cheese.

Elsewhere in mountainous Auvergne you meet the light red and white Ferrandaise cattle; in the lowlands of Allier are the heavy creamy-white Charolais.

In the old days, cowherds spent the summer with their cattle, living in the drystone *burons* where one room was for sleeping, another for making butter and cheese, and a third for storing the *fourmes* of cheese. The hard work and skill needed for this occupation is described by Pierre Besson (1873 - 1945), a native of Cheylade, in *Un Pâtre du Cantal* (1914). *Burons* are hardly used now; good roads and cars allow the cowherds to drive up daily to their herds. Not all *burons* were used for cheese making. In beef cattle areas a large landowner would let his *montagne* to small peasant-farmers from the valleys who sent their collective herds to these summer pastures. Payment was merely the fertilising dung left by the cattle.

Once, sheep were kept in larger numbers than now, though they are still moved great distances for the seasonal transhumance, leaving the arid plains of Bas-Languedoc for the fresh summer pastures of Auvergne. Not long ago, the transhumance was an epic journey on foot, up in June, down in October, a pattern of living that had endured for millennia. Now the sheep are transported by lorry.

*   *   *

The religious aspects of pastoralism retain much of their ancient vigour, as may be instanced by the ceremonies at Chapelle de la Font-Sainte, amidst the high pastures above Apchon in Cantal. The chapel was built in 1837 and later enlarged to make room for all the cattle men and shepherds who came to worship the Virgin. On July 2nd each year her effigy is carried from the church of St. Hippolyte to remain in the chapel until the end of September. The popular pilgrimages take place on the Feast of St. Anne at the end of July; again in mid-August; the last Thursday in August, which is the Feast of the Shepherds; and in early September.

*   *   *

Time was — and not long ago — when the whole world thought of the Auvergnat as wearing his traditional garb of black velvet hat, blue smock *(la biaude),* and sabots for the men; voluminous black skirts and shawls by the women. Such a sight is rare now, though sabots are certainly worn, and the Auvergnat beret is ubiquitous. You see them on market days — especially the early autumn cattle markets — which are male preserves for quizzing, bargaining, haggling, considering and finally settling the deal with gesticulations, handshakes and drinks.

Back in 1784 there were so many variants in local costumes that an author named Chabrol had to devote four volumes to describe them. A farmer's wife

70

might have had a star bonnet faced with silk and lingerie frill with a bow at the back. Her dress might have been of homespun wool; her apron of homespun cotton. Deep cuffs at her wrists; a shawl of cotton, block-printed in bright colours. Her stockings would be of knitted wool; her sabots heel-less.

A young woman of the Bourbonnais would be more elegantly dressed than her counterpart from Auvergne. Her dress of cloth had a velvet border of contrasting colours at the hem, and was covered by a cashmere shawl, sheer white apron with bib and hem edged with crochet lace. A dainty straw hat, almost cylindrical, faced and banded with velvet, with a bow-shaped rim over forehead and ears. Silver-buckled shoes were worn over black silk stockings.

*   *   *

Folklore groups have revived regional costumes, dances and old musical instruments. Though they no longer belong to daily life — they are museums-in-the-life of a dead past — they let the visitor see what costume and dance were like once upon a time, just as he can listen to the gramophone records of old 'Songs of Auvergne', sung by Victoria de los Angeles.

The Auvergnat *bourrée* dance has been famous all the world over for many years. Experts say the word does not derive from *bourrée*, 'a bundle of twigs', but from *bourrir*, 'to flap the wings'. I do not know why this should be, since such gestures are not part of the *bourrée* movements. It is nonetheless a true folk dance, a homage to the province, whose antiquity is hard to establish. It was not a society dance until the Bourbonnais version was introduced to court by Margaret, sister of King Charles IX, who reigned between 1560 and 1574. It was danced in honour of Catherine de Medici in 1565. In 1676, Madame de Sévigné wrote from Vichy that the *bourrée* was the most beautiful dance in the world, but it was not known at Versailles.

There are various regional *bourrées* whose figures vary. In Auvergne it is danced in 3/4 time, and is harsher and livelier than a waltz. Its beauty lies in the perfect execution of the *pas de bourrée* used throughout by couples revolving in a circle or chain. Basically simple, it is difficult to perform, as figures follow in rapid succession, in quick tempo. There exist the *Bourrée à quatre, Bourrée à deux, Bourrée de St. Flour* which has seven figures plus entree and sortie, and another *bourrée* from the Mauriac region.

In the 19th century it was considered by townspeople to be heavy and uncouth, as it was danced in sabots or hob-nailed boots, with a thumping stamp to mark each third beat. Today's versions are lively and graceful with rhythmic to-and-fro movements of the man's arms. Even so, the *bourrée* still reflects the reserved temperament of rural Auvergne, and is not a spectacular dance. As Peter Gorham says, 'music and dancing rather than literature is their cultural heritage'.

In its pure form, the *bourrée* is accompanied by the *vielle*, a squeakily droning,

Folk-dance group

two- or three- stringed hurdy-gurdy, sounded by a rosined wheel turned by the player's right hand. Keys at the other end of the short, lute-like instrument 'stop' the strings played with the left hand. In the castle at Montluçon is a valuable *vielle* museum. A fiddle player may accompany the *vielle;* a kind of bagpipe or *cabrette* can be brought in as well.

The Bourbonnais *bourrée* is danced in 2/4 and not 3/4 time. Its style is smoother, more languid, but the accompanying instruments are the same. This was the *bourrée* to spread to England as the *bore* or *borry* for which Purcell wrote music, as Rameau did in France. *La Bourrée fantasque* was a ballet created by Balanchine.

*   *   *

Traditional costumes are brought out for the procession of the Festival of St. Amable at Riom at ten in the morning, either on June 11th or the Sunday following. Peasants of the region, known as *Brayauds*, wear 17th century costumes of white, rough, homespun clothes, and a curious bicorned headdress. This ceremony is linked with a procession at Marsat which takes place on the Sunday after Ascension Day. In the church of Notre Dame — on the site of what may have been the first Marial shrine in France — is the sad, contemplative Black Virgin in Majesty. Suspended nearby is a three km roll of thin wax. The origin is that in 916, the town of Riom, three km away, was delivered from siege by Norman raiders. The Riomois vowed to the Virgin at Marsat thenceforward to offer her a thread of wax that stretched between the two places. Only the Revolution interrupted the ritual of the 'wheel of wax'. Today, one beflowered wheel of wax is carried at the Procession of the Brayauds at St. Amable in Riom, and another is taken to Marsat.

At Saugues in Haute-Loire, on Maundy Thursday, an intense and complex procession takes place at nightfall. White Penitents with staves and lanterns walk with red-cloaked Penitents, one of whose number carries the Cross.

Religious traditions throughout the province preserve the sense of continuity with processions in honour of local patronal saints, but the festivals associated with the Black Virgins whose origins will be discussed in the next chapter — are the most intense religious expressions of the Auvergnats.

Chief among them is the pilgrimage of Notre Dame des Miracles at Mauriac on the Sunday following May 9th. Large crowds follow the procession round Clermont-Ferrand when the little 13th century Black Virgin, copied from a Byzantine ikon, is taken from the altar of Notre Dame du Port. Orcival possesses Auvergne's finest Virgin in Majesty, carved in wood in the 12th century and covered with silver and gold. The procession is escorted by twelve barefoot priests, and is held on Ascension Day; torchlight processions and singing on the hills outside Orcival take place the previous night. At Besse-en-Chandesse, on July 2nd, the Black Virgin of Notre Dame de Vassivière is taken from St. André church to the chapel of Vassivière, seven km away. This is the *Fête de la Montée* (the ascent). She is brought back to Besse on the *Fête de la Dévalade* (the descent) on the Sunday after September 21st. This is a pastoral tradition, coinciding with the movement of flocks to summer pastures. Songs and prayers accompany the crowds making for the chapel, and when both the *Montée* and *Dévalade* are over, they dance and merrymake and let off fireworks.

*   *   *

Finally, a word about traditions which tourism is keeping alive. These are the practice of old crafts. Auvergne is noted for its craft holidays. Visitors can learn the old techniques, in some cases staying in cottages *en famille* with local craftsmen, or in a craft village. Obviously, one must be French-speaking. Courses are mostly held in summer and last seven, ten or fourteen days, and cover such diverse subjects as pottery, wood carving, weaving, painting on porcelain, music and painting. There are centres at Clermont-Ferrand, Aurillac, Riom, Loubaresse near St. Flour, Bas-en-Basset and Chambon-sur-Lignon.

8

A CORNUCOPIA OF CASTLES & CHURCHES

Two architectural legacies from the past enrich the traveller's pleasure in the present. They are the châteaux and the churches that are scattered liberally throughout the province.

First the châteaux, which you will start meeting as soon as you enter the Allier *département* from the north. I keep to the French word 'châteaux' because it can be conveniently used to embrace not only the medieval fortifications or 'castles', but also a whole variety of large and small manor houses and country seats which were built at a later date. Someone has calculated — and it would be difficult to verify — that more than 500 châteaux were built in Auvergne. A good percentage of these were feudal castles, reminders of Auvergne's turbulent and fragmented history in the Middle Ages. The rest are the elegant Renaissance (though the Renaissance developed late in Auvergne) country seats of the nobility, and the manor houses of the squires and wealthy bourgeoisie. Far less grand than the buildings of their contemporaries which made the fame of the château-country of the Loire valley, these in Auvergne are nonetheless numerous and attractive.

Auvergne runs the gamut of chateaux, from the grotto strongholds as at Jonas, or medieval fortresses such as Châteaugay, to the elegant 18th century Château de Parentignat which bears the sobriquet, *'le petit Versailles'*; from the romantically turretted, water-girt Château du Val in Cantal (though the lake setting is recent and man made), to the much photographed fortress of La Voûte-Polignac in Haute-Loire. There is the dainty little Château de la Salle in Allier, as well as the same *département's* Château de Fourchaud, one of the loveliest 14th century fortresses in Bourbonnais which looks ideally suited to its present use as a farm.

For the medieval barons, Auvergne's terrain provided ready-made sites on which to build defensive castles. A hundred pinnacles of basalt and humps of bare lava asked to be used as commanding positions from which were uninterrupted vistas that gave far more than four-minute warnings of approaching assailants.

Most of these castles are in ruins now, mouldering picturesquely on their

Ruins of the Château at Arlempdes

eminences. It was not only time which pulled down their walls. As social conditions changed, they became redundant and fell into disrepair; many were destroyed and not rebuilt during the Hundred Years War; peasants hostile to the freebooting captains who had taken over empty castles, pulled them down and used the stone for constructing their own homes. Or else the castles were systematically dismantled on the orders of Cardinal Richelieu in his determination to bring order to the region; and finally, the French Revolution delivered the *coup de grâce* in the extirpation of the nobility.

Some châteaux are well-known and much visited; others are merely chanced upon and glimpsed from the roadside. Some are hemmed in by modern towns; others have a village clustered at their feet, a mother duck gathering her unruly brood underneath her. Other buildings stand alone; they seem to invite the passer-by to invent a history for them.

One of the best known and most photographed is the Château de Tournoël, a little northwest of Clermont-Ferrand, and just outside Volvic. The castle ruins sit aloft on a cone, above the sweet-chestnut trees, and look over the Limagne valley and the Allier river and the town of Riom. Its story is illustrative of the fate of many other châteaux hereabouts.

It may have been built as early as the 11th century by the Counts of Auvergne. The King, Philippe Auguste, on a punitive raid into Auvergne, destroyed the building in 1213. The ruins visible today are the remains of a new castle begun in the 13th century and greatly strengthened in the following century. During the Wars of Religion it was attacked unsuccessfully but badly battered. Then, in 1632, it was captured by Gaston d'Orléans in his struggle against Richelieu. In consequence, Tournoël was specially marked out for destruction; Richelieu and Louis XIII partly destroyed it. Neglect, wind and weather hastened the deterioration. In 1766, what was left was bought by Guillaume de Chabrol; the same family still owns it and is slowly restoring the romantic medieval fortress, which consists of a square keep and a tall, circular tower, defensive walls and turrets, and a courtyard surrounded by the main group of medieval buildings.

*   *   *

Chateau de la Barge, Puy de Dôme

It is the churches of the Romanesque period which are of outstanding interest, because the Romanesque style developed along its own lines in Auvergne. Some of the churches are large and famous — Notre Dame du Port in Clermont-Ferrand, Issoire, Orcival and St. Nectaire, for example. Others are small rural churches. There are about 250 buildings of this period extant in Auvergne, and the period to which Auvergnat Romanesque refers is the 11th and 12th centuries.

The word 'Romanesque' crops up constantly in any reference to French medieval architecture, and so it may be useful to trace the evolution of this important phase in the history of building, a phase whose style is, in the eyes of

Polignac, the Castle and the Church

The Chateau at Cordès (Puy de Dôme)

many, impressive and beautiful. There were, of course, many local blendings and variations of the style, of interest to the student. We need concern ourselves here only with the blueprint, as it were, of the ecclesiastical buildings erected between the 11th and 13th centuries. A short flowering, then, of the Romanesque, for it was supplanted by another technical advance in church architecture, the Gothic.

What we in English call Romanesque (and which roughly equates with Norman) is in French *roman*. A more strictly appropriate translation of *roman* would be Romance, because the style derived directly from Roman models, though infused with a new artistic spirit before the development of Gothic. As I have said, we tend to call pre-Gothic styles Norman, but this does not really cover all the Romanesque styles imported into England.

France had at least six distinct schools of pre-Gothic architecture: Norman, Burgundian, Poitevin, Périgourdin, Provençal and Auvergnat. For all of them the Roman basilica was the prototype. In ancient Rome, the basilica was a large, simple, oblong building used as a lawcourt or exchange. At the east end, in a semi-circular recess, sat the tribune and judge. Over the arches of a nave, vestibule and aisles were the galleries of the triforium. A simple wooden roof of low pitch covered the building.

At first, the plan of the Roman basilica required little conversion to suit the needs of Christian worship. The tribune became the apse in front of which was placed the altar. As other semi-circular chapels were added, the apsidal east end came to be known as the chevet. Ambo and choir were ranged in the centre of the nave, and the vestibule at the west end opposite the tribune became the narthex. The Christian cross was inserted with the transept.

Before Romanesque emerged, there had been, in the 8th and 9th centuries, a

Church of Notre Dame du Port, Clermont-Ferand

Carolingian architecture. This followed the dictates of Charlemagne who either copied or else actually appropriated parts of more ancient buildings, but no complete examples of Carolingian architecture remain in Auvergne.

Charlemagne's empire collapsed into the chaos of lack of central authority and an insufficient production of food. Famine and epidemics returned again and again. Great areas of Europe's countryside were terrorised by parasitic robbers. Despair was widespread, and misery expressed itself in the belief that the year 1000 would see the end of the world. The fateful year came and went and hope began to reassert itself. There was, as it happened, an Auvergnat pope at Rome, and the First Crusade was launched from Clermont-Ferrand.

French architects at the beginning of the second millennium caught the new mood of optimism; they became imbued with a spirit of innovation which wanted to create a new ecclesiastical architecture. The old seemed no longer apposite.

There were technical difficulties. How did you vault a basilica with stone, while yet creating buildings with a sense of space, light and elevation? The Italians, with their light wooden roofs, had little difficulty in raising the inner walls of the nave and piercing them with windows. But if the workers with stone roofs tried the same thing, the thrust from the roof's barrel-vaults on top of the nave threatened to burst the walls outwards the moment the clerestory was opened to put in windows. It took two hundred years before the proper solution was found — rib-vaulting and flying buttresses, the Gothic solution. The Romanesque never found the proper answers.

All French Romanesque schools were trying to bring direct light to the central space of the church. The Normans evaded the problem by retaining the wooden roof; the Burgundians were so bold that the church at Cluny fell down more than once, and others almost did so. In Auvergne, innate conservatism led to the retention of the blind nave, as well as blind arcades that connected the outer buttresses of the nave; the aisles were often two-storeyed and were used, perhaps, for storing valuables brought back by Crusaders or pilgrims. Churches in Auvergne are also noted for the inlay work with polychrome stone, usually as a band round the outside of the choir. A very ancient tradition was often followed, by which a mosaic decoration was made with pebbles encrusted in mortar. You see this round the roof and apsidal chapels of Notre Dame du Port at Clermont-Ferrand.

The middle portion of the transept is raised into a box-like upper storey on which the often two-storeyed octagonal tower is supported. The western tower is rectangular. Round the ambulatory, chapels radiate like a cluster of martins' nests. Where volcanic stone has been used, Auvergnat churches are variously coloured with seams of dark yellow, brown and other colours, the whole giving an effect of sombreness.

Why should the Romanesque architects have insisted on stone roofs which gave them such headaches for close on two hundred years? They were determined to reduce fire hazards, and, more importantly, they wanted places of worship which served also as defensive fortresses. This need often arose. The need was frequently engineered by Crusaders returning from the wars, practising the lawlessness with which they had often fought their way to the Holy Land. At that time, then, the role of the Church in sparsely populated and unprotected areas was to be an oasis of shelter, a centre of teaching, and the upholder of local government.

Other Crusaders brought back oriental ideas; the churches of western France — Périgord in particular — are strongly oriental in character; Périgueux or Angouleme look from a distance like little Jerusalems with their domed churches, although, in point of fact, this oriental influence had already been brought to western Europe before the start of the First Crusade. Auvergne lay a little to one side of the mainstream of this Byzantine influence, but Mozarab themes do occur in a number of churches there. An example is Chauriat in Puy-de-Dôme, where a highly original stone marquetry decorates the south facade. The Byzantine-Poitou style reasserts itself in Velay. Experts say that the structure of the dome at Le Puy-en-Velay shows a direct Persian influence.

The Auvergnat Romanesque school, founded even before the beginning of the 11th century in the diocese of Clermont, did not confine itself to the province. As with other Romanesque schools, it had offshoots further afield in France, and even as far away as Santiago de Compostella in Spain, and St. John's Chapel in the Tower of London. It reached its zenith in the early years of the 12th century. Solemn, forbidding, massively impressive with a heavy boldness from the outside, this style seems to me to bear the hallmark of a truculent Christianity whose God was to be looked for almost at ground level. For eye and mind seem drawn earthwards rather than heavenwards by the squat, bulging impregnability of the castles of God responsible for the defence of the populace huddled at their feet.

In the Bourbonnais, the styles of Auvergne and Burgundy meet — as does secular architecture in the solid farmhouses. In Cantal, the churches are smaller, and the main regional characteristic is the flat belfry-wall within which are suspended a row of bells beneath sheltering arch openings, a feature which recurs in Provence.

*   *   *

For the human touch of charm or even a kind of minatory wit, one has to turn to the smaller scale of decorative carvings and frescoes. Most Romanesque churches will have had their walls painted originally, but not many survive. Those at Issoire are poor restorations or imitations. Frescoes painted in the church at Chasteloy in the Aumance valley, dated between the 13th and 17th centuries, are also restored. Those at Novacelles, says Peter Gorham,

The Chapel of St. Michel, Le Puy

though Romanesque in style, were probably painted later. But at Saulcet (Allier), the murals are fine; they were started in the 12th century, ending with a 14th century Christ in Majesty.

The early Church was torn between the iconoclasts who condemned everything that was not austere, and those who saw in ecclesiastical decoration, whether pictorial or sculptural, a means of teaching and uplifting. This latter function was expressed with eloquence by Gregory the Great, pope between 590 and 604, in a condemnation of the iconoclasts. 'It is one thing to worship a picture and another to learn from the language of a picture what that is which ought to be worshipped. What those who can, learn by means of writing, that do the uneducated learn by looking at a picture'.

To this same end, the Romanesque builders, nearly five hundred years after Pope Gregory, wanted to decorate churches in France with glass cube mosaics in the way Byzantine artists had succeeded in making their churches glow, rich and sumptuous, in the half light. French craftsmen lacked the skill; they made do with paint or distemper. They were poor, and there were many churches for them to decorate.

The uneducated were most effectively taught through the three-dimensional solidity of carving, and of sculptors in France there were many. At first they merely copied Roman capitals and sarcophagi whose themes were made appropriately Christian. Later, an indigenous style emerged, and Auvergne produced one of the earliest.

True, Auvergne produced no carved portals of the manificence of Arles and St. Gilles in Provence, for example, where the religious messages of sin, damnation and redemption thundered from the silent stone of the tympanum on the eyes of the pilgrims making their way along the *Via Podensis* to Santiago de Compostella in Spain, the third most important of all medieval pilgrimages. The first was to Jerusalem, the second to Rome, but the one to Santiago de Compostella became the most popular.

Auvergne's carved messages on the outside of its pilgrim churches are more modest. There is, for instance, the tympanum at Chambon-du-Lac. There is the side portal of Notre Dame du Port in Clermont-Ferrand, which has a saddle-back lintel depicting the vision of the prophet Isiah; above it is the dominating high-relief of Christ in Majesty. All these figures were mutilated during the French Revolution. The tympanum of Notre Dame des Miracles at Mauriac in Cantal is in a purely Languedocian style.

A truer expression of Romanesque Auvergnat individuality is to be found within the churches rather than without. Sculpting of capitals came before carving round the outside doors. In a number of churches the light is too poor to distinguish much detail. In others, the lively scenes from the Old and New Testaments, the themes with regional allusions and local saints, the fantastical figures and symbols, are more easily seen. Sometimes the carvings have been executed with skill, refinement and a nice sense of humour. Elsewhere, the work is rough and crude. At Châtel-Montagne in Allier, where the hard granite must have given the chisel the utmost difficulty, the acrobatic Atlantes look for all the world like the primitive carvings of the Celto-Ligurian tribes in Provence, a thousand years earlier. So do the archaic 11th century sculptured capitals in the church at Thuret in Puy-de-Dôme.

One theme to be repeatedly emphasised in the carvings on Auvergnat capitals is the condemnation of the vice of usury; Ennezat (Puy-de-Dôme) provides a good example.

*   *   *

Auvergnat sculpture, Chapel of St Michel

Two other aspects of Auvergnat sculpture commend themselves. One is the figure carvings, mostly in wood, often encrusted with gold leaf or copper sheeting and precious stones. Fingers and feet are emphasised by being greatly elongated; the eyes are dark and large, staring and almond-shaped. In Cantal especially, almost every church has a Virgin or saint carved in this curiously stylised, oriental manner. Best known, perhaps, is the image of St. Baudime in the treasury at St. Nectaire, a beautifully executed gold-plated bust by a Limousin artist of the 12th century.

The other aspect of church decoration is the celebrated Black Virgins of Auvergne. They are similarly stylised, and many are still venerated; some of the major pilgrimage centres were mentioned in the previous chapter.

The effect on the onlooker of these stylised figures is pronounced. Aloof and inviolable, their eyes seem to gaze through and beyond us. There is no concession to prettiness and sentimentality; they seem to embody the very spirit of quietism.

One of the most expressive of them all is the Virgin in Majesty in Notre Dame de Claviers at Jailhac in Cantal, carved in the 11th century.

Why these carvings should be painted black is uncertain, but the oriental connection again seems self-evident. One is reminded of the patron saint of the gypsies who are thought to have come from Egypt — the black Sara in the church of Les Saintes-Maries-de-la-Mer in the Camargue. One thinks, too, of the original Black Virgin of Le Puy-en-Velay, who was burned during the Revolution. She had been carved out of dark cedar wood and swathed in bands of papyrus. The story goes that she had been found by St. Louis on his Crusade in Egypt in the middle of the 13th century, and presented by him to Le Puy. As one writer has put it, she had 'a suspiciously Egyptian appearance', and could well have been an Egyptian idol representing Isis and the infant Horus. However true that may be, hers became an important cult, and chapels dedicated to the Virgin of Le Puy dot the pilgrim route to Spain.

Some wooden Mother and Child statues of the Romanesque period — not only in Auvergne but elsewhere in France, too — were painted black, and have been repainted many times since. Others were left in the natural dark wood and have darkened still further with the dirt, wax and candle heat of the years, to say nothing of having been burned by accident and design.

Surely one is in the presence, yet again, of Byzantium in France, that powerful stream whose distant origins were in Persia, slowly to migrate westwards along trade routes, bringing religious, architectural, sculptural and decorative influences. All along the way, local ideas were modified. Finally, this stream came as far west as France, as far north as Scandinavia.

In the artistic metamorphosis wrought by two centuries of the Romanesque, the most impressive carvings are those figures which embody simple devotion, whose postures suggest stillness and humility, before the grandiose, the theatrical and the sentimental gained ascendancy in religious art. The best of the Romanesque was an inwardness which in stone or wood seemed to understand the most profound of human longing.

9

THE AUVERGNATS AS OTHERS SEE THEM

Who is a 'typical' Auvergnat? Pierre Laval, perhaps? Or the President of France, Valéry Giscard d'Estaing? Or Julius Caesar's doughty adversary, Vercingètorix? All are sons of Auvergne. Is there some characteristic common to them all which makes one say, 'Of course, typical Auvergnats!'? Probably not.

National and regional stereotypes are easily conjured, and the Auvergnat stereotype is no exception. To some extent, the image has been built up from those émigrés, the poor boys who left to work in hotels in Vichy, or fended as best they might as unskilled workers in Paris — rag-and-bone men, coal-merchants, roast-chestnut vendors, barmen.

From literary sources we have the image of a shrewd, hard-working peasant, careful to the point of meanness, monosyllabic save with those he knows, suspicious, easy to take offence. He is stocky, short-headed — brachycephalic, in technical jargon — with a broad, brown face.

You see men answering that description in the streets; short, elderly men in dark suits, wearing black straw hats or black berets, and speaking a gutteral sort of French. Their country's past hardships seem carved into set faces, faces whose brown complexion is touched with a grey as of volcanic lava.

This physical description bears no relation to the spare, elegant figure of Valéry Giscard d'Estang, once deputy for the Puy-de-Dôme and mayor of Chamalières, later President of France, not actually born in Auvergne, but with a long, aristocratic family connection with the province, himself the proponent of a liberal-conservative political philosophy. Nor does the description match another Auvergnat who, in fusing science with theology, has left a strong imprint on present-day thinking, Pierre Teilhard de Chardin. He had a long, expressive, mobile and luminously intelligent face.

Rightly or wrongly, a stereotype vision does fit Pierre Laval who, to many of an older generation, seemed to symbolise the evil of the pre-war years and the war years themselves, when he was the compliant creature of the victorious Nazis.

His political career has already been sketched. Perhaps more should now be said about Laval, the Auvergnat. He was born in 1883 in the captivating little town of Châteldon, off the main road between Vichy and Thiers, whose civic crest reads *Chastel oudon — petite ville à grand renom.* Son of a butcher-innkeeper and organiser of the local courrier service, he was short, heavy-featured, thick-lipped and swarthy. His eyes were black and flashing. These almost Levantine features he acquired from his mother. At school, young Laval displayed a sardonic humour; he played to win and dominate. His temper was violent and uncertain; he played cruel, practical jokes, was a gang leader, a rebel, and constantly fighting. He studied for the bar, and he built up a successful practice in Paris before going into politics in which he remained untouched by material corruption.

Unattractive in many ways, with dark, oily hair hanging over his right eye, tobacco-stained moustache and teeth, he learned to control his temper and developed a profound horror of violence. Yet he in no way lost his physical and moral courage. His apologists see in the transformation of his temper the reason for his decision to collaborate with the occupying Germans, for out of his wilder self had grown a wily negotiator, a supreme compromiser. He was an astute businessman who counted every *sou* and haggled over every *sou*, and paid the lowest wages. He married the daughter of the mayor of Châteldon; his own daughter married Count Réne de Chambrun, descendant of La Fayette, another well remembered Auvergnat. Pierre Laval retained the essential peasant reflexes, and a passionate love of his homeland.

With the defeat of the Germans in 1945, Laval's own fate — as he himself clearly foresaw — was quickly sealed. His trial, his attempted suicide, followed by immediate execution by firing squad, was all pathos, squalor and brutishness. What human dignity was left was Laval's. It is easy, and far too simple, to vilify the man. Laval the realist, was cast — and knew himself to be cast — as the dragon to de Gaulle's lofty St. George. The one cannot play out his role without the other; each played his part in the unfolding of a myth as old as mankind. Laval had to be sacrificed to begin the atonement for the guilt of occupation.

And Laval's Auvergne experienced its full share of resistance and collaboration and *épuration* — that mixture of purge and revenge, of self-justification and denigration. If Laval was 'typical' of anything Auvergnat, how 'typical' is the now elderly farmer of St. Yvoine near Issoire? He served with the Resistance, was betrayed to the Gestapo by a fellow-villager, suffered great hardships in the concentration camp before he could return to St. Yvoine, where he, and the man who denounced him, live today. He knows who denounced him. With a shoulder-shrug he asks what purpose would be served by revealing the man's name.

†   *   ⁕

The first Auvergnat figure in history was cast in the de Gaulle hero-mould, at least by subsequent patriots. Julius Caesar in his *Conquest of Gaul* found the

Arverni tribe to be brave, impetuous, ingenious, but without steadiness. They were, he said, given to treachery and bribery. The one opponent who commanded Caesar's respect was the Arvernian leader, Vercingetorix, commander-in-chief of the Gauls. We have his likeness on coins. Skill, foresight and authority were the qualities Caesar attributed to him.

There was also a Laval among the Arvernian commanders. Caesar names him as Epasnactus, and mentions one or two other Arvernians. One was Critognatus who urged his men not to surrender but to eat the flesh of those too old or young to fight.

Vercingetorix, who inflicted on Caesar his single reverse at Gergovia in 52 B.C., has an equestrian statue in Place de Jaude in Clermont-Ferrand, sculpted by Bartholdy who was responsible for the Statue of Liberty in New York harbour. On the Plateau de Gergovie is a twenty-six metre high monument of Volvic lava, put up in 1900, to the Gallic leader.

Emperor Napoleon III, who had the Gergovia site excavated from 1860 on, was an ardent admirer of Julius Caesar. Such are the quirks of history that those who were politically hostile towards the Emperor identified themselves with Vercingetorix. 'From this period can be dated the propensity of the French to identify themselves with their Gallic ancestors, to detect in them some of their own traditional failings, and to surround the great battles of Caesar's campaigns with something of the glamour they have always built up round the great defeats of their history'. This, it may be noted, is a quotation from the French archaeologist J.J. Hatt, in his Celts and Gallo-Romans.

Now we live in a period of anti-heroism. Out of the Auvergnat Vercingetorix, not long ago seen as heroic liberator and unifier of the nation, has metamorphosed the comic strip cartoon figure of Asterix and other Gaulish warriors. Their slapstick victories are won by wits and stealth against different adversaries than the soldier Caesar.

*   *   *

Between hero and anti-hero archetypes are ordinary people. English literature gives us a number of pen portraits of unidentified rural Auvergnats. The Reverend Sabine Baring-Gould was in Velay in 1907, and saw the upland peasants thus in A Book of the Cévennes: '. . . of medium height, is strongly built and of a vigorous constitution. Accustomed from childhood to follow his sheep and oxen in their leisurely movements, he also becomes a being of slow habit of body and even slower of mind. He is shy, timorous, and cautious of compromising himself in any way with his neighbours, above all with officials'.

I read Robert Louis Stevenson's Travels with a Donkey in the Cévennes, written in 1878, with never failing pleasure. Yet he must have behaved with abominable boorishness towards the people of Velay when he berates them for their uncouthness. Little wonder. This passage reveals his disrespect of their courtesy:

'At the bridge of Langogne a lassie of some seven or eight addressed me in the sacramental phrase, "D'où 'st que vous venez?" She did it with so high an air that she set me laughing; and this cut her to the quick. She was evidently one who reckoned on respect, and stood looking at me in silent dudgeon as I crossed the bridge'. An object-lesson, here, for thoughtless, arrogant tourists!

Going back further in time, comes this little vignette by Louise Stuart Costello in *A Pilgrimage to Auvergne* in 1842:

'They are a strange wild race, fond of money, avaricious, yet well off, extremely uneducated and coarse in their manners, easily excited, and somewhat brutal in their habits'.

There speaks a well-bred English lady. Much more understanding lies in the up-to-date *Portrait of the Auvergne* (1975) by Peter Gorham, who notes how the reticence of the landscape is mirrored in the sharp, ironic temper of the people, their friendliness that offsets the cool suspicion of the stranger, and their honesty.

The description I like best, because it has perception, balance and depth — apart from its beautiful writing — comes from George Sand whose native Berry abuts the Bourbonnais of northwestern Auvergne. She wrote of the Auvergnats in the mid-nineteenth century when the peasants still wore distinctive costums. This is Baring-Gould's translation:

'I find here a race very marked in its characteristics, altogether in harmony with the soil that supports it; meagre, gloomy, rough, and angular in its forms and in its instincts. At the tavern every one has his knife in his belt, and he drives the point into the lower face of the table, between his legs; after that they talk, they drink, they contradict one another, they become excited, and they fight. The houses are of an incredible dirtiness. The ceiling, made up of a number of strips of wood, serves as a receptacle for all their food and for all their rags. Alongside with their faults, I cannot but recognise some great qualities. They are honest and proud. There is nothing servile in the manner in which they receive you, with an air of frankness and genuine hospitality. In their innermost soul they partake of the beauties and the asperities of their climate and their soil.'

10

SOME MAKERS OF AUVERGNE

After Caesar's *Conquest of Gaul* had broadcast the first Auvergnat names of Vercingetorix and some of his lieutenants, the next figure concerns the slow evangelisation of the region which centred on Clermont-Ferrand. This was St. Austremoine or Stremonius who was sent from Rome with six other evangelists to convert Gaul to Christianity in 250. He preached to the Arverni, became the first bishop of Clermont, and was martyred at Issoire, *Icidorum* then, where the great church today bears his name. But St. Austremoine may not have been a native of Auvergne.

We know more about the character of Sidonius Apollinaris who lived between 430 and 489. He came of an illustrious Gallic family, was born in Lyon, and became governor and later bishop of *Arvernum* (Clermont) from 471 until his death. He was a man of all-round distinction — in science, literature, poetry and oratory, although his political record was less than fortunate.

The letters written by Sidonius have been preserved, and give valuable glimpses into the daily life of Auvergne in those times. We have a description in verse of his villa named *Avitacum* after his father-in-law, on the shore of Lac d'Aydat. An islet near the north bank is known as Ile de St. Sidoine in his memory. He calls his house modest, enjoying views of the hills and across the lake. The nearby woodlands supply him with timber for the furnace which heats his bath. A large indoor pool is roofed over and has seats around it, and there is an outdoor bathing pool as well. The house is of local stone and painted white. There are outhouses, women's quarters, and a summerhouse. Sidonius relates how he sits drinking snow-cooled wine while watching the fishermen out in the lake. He describes the rural sounds of frogs, chickens, swans, geese, a whole variety of wild birds, cattle, cowbells and shepherds' pipes.

A picture drawn straight out of Virgil's *Georgics*, one could imagine, and typical of the luxury which nobles enjoyed even as the Roman Empire moved to its fall in the west, and even as the Visigoths were already mastering Auvergne; *'a race of uncivilised allies directs the Roman power, yes, and bids fair to bring it crashing to the ground'*, wrote Sidonius in tones which can only be described as those of a complacent hedonist. He loved Auvergne, and wrote of it, *'pastures*

crown the hilltops and vineyards clothe the slopes . . . villas rise on the lowlands and castles on the rocks, forests here and clearings there, valleys with springs, headlands washed by rivers. . . .'

Half a century later appears the historian and bishop of Clermont, where he was born — Gregory of Tours (538-594). He wrote the early Christian history of Auvergne, and is best remembered for his ten books, *Historia Francorum,* the early part of which deals with the creation of the world by drawing largely on legend and tradition. In writing of contemporary events he becomes a quaintly valuable source of reference, in spite of the evident shakiness of his geography.

A major medieval figure was Gerbert, born of peasant stock in the village of Belliac near Aurillac in 940. He was to become the first French pope as Pope Sylvester II, in 999, to die in 1003. His statue in Aurillac is by David d'Angers, and a stele at Belliac commemorates him. After being taught by the monks of Aurillac, Gerbert went to Spain and studied mathematics and medicine at Arab universities. On his return to France he taught at Rheims, where he became such a brilliant teacher that scholars from all over Europe came to sit at his feet, for he introduced originality and depth of thought to the subjects he discoursed on, without any sacrifice of discipline. He revolutionised the medieval system of education, and paved the way for the splendours of the 12th century 'renaissance'. By introducing Europe for the first time to the nine Hindu-Arabic numerals, and reviving the use of the abacus, he made the mechanics of counting easy. Music, astronomy, logic and rhetoric all bore signs of his original influence. He constructed the first clock with weights, invented an astrolabe, and improved the manufacture of organs. Such a diversity of skills brought hostility. Contemporaries suspected him of possessing the power to conjure demons; they called him a magician and a sorcerer. Even his elevation to the papacy was said to have been achieved by demonic assistance, but then, any man in those days who concerned himself with Arabic learning ran the risk of opprobrium.

In his written works, especially in *Correspondence,* Gerbert remembered with affection and gratitude the abbey at Aurillac where his formative years were spent. He was the pontiff in Rome in the doom-laden year 1000, the year when all medieval Europe believed the world would end. As the world survived, Gerbert ruled as pope for three more years into the period of renewed optimism.

*   *   *

The Roman Empire had imposed Latin as the upper class, administrative and religious language on the whole of Gaul south of the Loire. Side by side with

Issoire, Puy de Dôme

pure Latin existed the speech of the common people, made up of remnants of a Celtic language and bits of Greek and Latin. With the invasion of the Goths, Latin lost its status; the rustic tongue came into its own to be used by all classes, to become identified as the occitan *langue d'oc* of the south as distinct from the francien *langue d'oïl* of the north, in which both *oc* and *oïl* meant *'oui'* or 'yes'. In the 13th century, the *langue d'oïl* became the official written language and so established itself as the French language almost as it is today.

The *langue d'oc*, between the 11th and 13th centuries, became the language of the troubadours, the Provençal *trobador* from *trobar clar*, 'the clear invention'. Provence, Aquitaine and Limousin are the regions most closely identified with

the rise of the troubadours. Auvergne, too, had its troubadour tradition by which the wandering poet-singers entertained the seigneurial houses and 'courts of love' which were considered particularly refined in Auvergne — a little surprising, perhaps, in view of the unruly history of that period.

The Auvergnat troubadours are shadowy figures. Pierre d'Auvergne of Clermont, son of a bourgeois family and a presentable young man, sang well and wrote fine poetry with fair ease in the 12th century. He found favour with the families of noble barons, living to a ripe old age, and becoming the bishop of Clermont. He was among the earliest troubadours.

A little later came Hughes de Peirols (1160-1225) whose voice and poetic skill were much admired at one of the great centres, Chateau de Montferrand, where the Dauphin d'Auvergne held literary court. The 'Monk of Montadon', Pierre de Vic (1145-1220), born at Castel-Vieil de Vic, where one of the village streets bears his name, sang at the courts of Philippe Auguste, the King of Aragon and Richard Coeur de Lion (himself a famous troubadour whose best-known pieces were composed when in captivity and were addressed to his sister, the Countess of Toulouse); Pierre de Vic gained the highest honours in the literary 'courts of love'.

Both writers and troubadours from Velay were active beyond the confines of the province. Pierre Cardenal (1180-1278) was the best known. He was born at Le Puy and was one of the most vigorous of all medieval satirists, and about

Château de Tournoel, Puy de Dôme

sixty-six of his poems survive. Pons de Chapteuil and Raymond d'Aiguille were two other troubadours of the period.

The songs of the troubadours were written within a framework of strict conventions, both of style and content. They reflected the feudal relationships — the mutual bonds and obligations — between seigneur and vassal. For the most part, love songs were formal, flattering, ritual exaggerations that recognised the singer's fealty. They do not concern a real passion or a real person. They are stereotyped and sophisticated persona, the mask that allowed the singer to reach the top of the medieval pops. Commercial success was important in this precarious occupation. The protestations of love, then, had as much sexual significance as a kiss on the Queen's hand during a royal ceremony. True, a few poems did permit a speculation on the bedworthiness of certain ladies. Some poems were composed and sung by women troubadours, best known of whom was 'la Dame du Castel d'Auze', born around 1205, whose songs made the Château d'Auze at Senezergues, just in Aveyron from Montsalvy, famous.

*   *   *

A leap of 500 years brings us to a genius of Auvergnat birth, Blaise Pascal (1623-62). The house in which he was born in Rue des Gras in Clermont-Ferrand was pulled down in 1958, and only an inscription marks the site. A street and a square in the city are named after him; in the latter is a bronze statue of him on a marble pedestal. The model for it can be seen in the Salle Blaise Pascal in Musée du Ranquet. Here also is his portrait, and that of his sister. The calculating machine he invented, with the family crest on it, is also displayed.

By the age of sixteen he showed his mathematical genius by publishing a *Geometry of Conics* (1639), a work which astonished Descartes. Two years later he invented the calculating machine. He then devised a two-wheeled carriage, and thought up an idea which was to be adopted by the Paris omnibuses: coaches to ply between stated places at regular intervals for fixed fares.

In 1648 Pascal was in Paris. He asked his brother-in-law, Perier, to test Toricelli's hypothesis that the weight of air caused a column of mercury to rise. Would Perier measure a column of mercury in Clermont-Ferrand, and another on top of the Puy de Dôme? Perier was able to report that at 1,465m the column registered 8.4cm less than the one at Clermont. Thus was it proved that air had weight.

Apart from mathematical and natural scientific work, Pascal's writings as a philosopher and theologian had a great impact, for they were some of the most lucid French prose had seen.

With subtle irony and wit he wrote *The Provincial Letters* in 1656-57 after he had retired to Port-Royal to adopt the ascetic way of life of the Jansenists (as his sister had done). This religious system was based on the teachings of Bishop Cornelius Jansen (1585-1638) of Ypres, which maintained that human will, being perverse and incapable of good, can only love God by conversion, and that God converts whom He pleases. Pascal did not justify his faith by reasoning; he said 'The heart has its reasons, of which reason is ignorant'. *The Provincial Letters* were condemned by Pope Alexander VII in 1657, and publicly burned in 1660, but Pascal remained faithful to the Roman Catholic church. Rationalists would say, no doubt, that he sacrificed his intellect for his God. In this there is some parallel in the life of a more recent Auvergnat, Teilhard de Chardin, which I shall come to shortly.

Pascal's *Pensées* were published posthumously in 1670, and exercised a profound influence on theologians. In this work he emerges as a very modern man in his intellectual detachment, his quick thinking, his impatience and peevishness. He is a pessimist — perhaps on account of constant ill-health and his near deformity — and one can sense the attraction of the Jansenist view of life for a man who turned an hostile outlook upon himself. In doing so, he revelled in paradox. Human misery, he says, is assuaged solely by distractions, yet distractions are our greatest misery because they make us lose contact with ourselves. All our troubles stem from restlessness; we are unable to remain quiet and alone with ourselves in a room. Yet our nature is essentially dedicated to movement; total repose is death. And Pascal says somewhere that if we could read other men's thoughts, friendship would be destroyed.

A century later, another writer, also born at Clermont-Ferrand, Nicolas Sébastien Roch, known as Chamfort (1740-94), is remembered for his cynical aphorisms and satirical anecdotes. In Paris he identified himself with a revolutionary movement, but, threatened with arrest during the Terror, committed suicide.

*   *   *

Of military heroes Auvergne has produced its fair share. Antoine Coiffier-Ruzé, Marquis d'Effiat (1581-1632), was a Marshal of France, Superintendant of Finances, and friend of Richelieu. Duc de Villars (1653-1734); Duke of Berwick (1670 1734), natural son of James II by the sister of the Duke of Marlborough, also became a Marshal of France, and was born at Moulins; Admiral d'Orvilliers (1708-92); Admiral Charles-Henri d'Estaing (1729-94), scion of a distinguished family, defeated the English to capture the island of Grenada in the West Indies in 1779, and was executed at the Revolution; General Desaix (1768-1800) served Napoleon in Egypt and was killed at Marengo; while Marshal Fayolle commanded the Sixth French Army on the Somme in 1916.

One of the great masters of the art of war in the 17th century was Marshal Turenne (1611-75), whose family name of La Tour d'Auvergne had been associated with that village since the 13th century. He distinguished himself during the Thirty Years War, against the Fronde rebellion, and against the Spanish in the Netherlands. He also gave French school textbooks a resounding quota-

Château de Ravel, Puy de Dôme

tion, that 'Frenchmen could neither rest nor sleep as long as a single German remained in Alsace'.

A more equivocal figure for the historian to assess is the Marquis de La Fayette (1757-1834). He was born at the Château of Chavaniac-Lafayette which now belongs to the American 'La Fayette Memorial' and contains a 1914-18 War museum, as well as a little museum of the library and room where La Fayette was born. He is honoured by Americans for his part in the struggle of the colonists to gain independence. The idea so fired him that he fitted out a vessel, landed at Charleston in 1777, got himself wounded at Brandywine, commanded a division, brought reinforcements from France, and rendered diplomatic services to the American cause.

After representing the nobility of Auvergne in the States-General in 1789, he fell foul of the Revolution — he had what might be called right-wing views with which he nonetheless betrayed his king — and was formally declared a traitor and had to flee France. Back he came in 1799, and sat in the Chamber of Deputies for the rest of his life, returning once more to America in 1824 amid scenes of wild enthusiasm.

La Fayette must be dubbed brave, vain and stupid. Nor do all Frenchmen see him as the romantic liberator some Americans make him out to be. Nor did Thomas Carlyle who, in his *French Revolution*, called La Fayette 'this constitutional pedant, clear, thin, inflexible, as water turned to ice'.

In the political field Auvergne has produced its Laval, who has been discussed at length. The province has given France two presidents: Giscard d'Estaing, as we have seen, and Paul Doumer (1857-1932). He was a native of Aurillac, was made president in 1931 in preference to Aristide Briand, and

Marquis d'Effiat (1581-1632)

assassinated in May of the following year by a mad Russian; a president about whom the historians find little to say.

* * *

Clermont-Ferrand has always been the religious and intellectual heart of Auvergne. Its industrial importance began in 1832. Two cousins, Aristide Barbier and Edouard Daubrée, set up a little shop making agricultural implements. Daubrée's wife was the niece of the inventive Scottish chemist, Charles Macintosh. He, having discovered that rubber dissolves in benzine, applied the principle commercially by lining cloth with indiarubber to make waterproof clothing — macintoshes. The process was patented in 1823.

Drawing on family ingenuity, Madame Daubrée made rubber balls for her children to play with. Her husband then manufactured and sold them, as well as other articles requiring rubber, in the Clermont shop. At first, prosperity; then the business decayed until the use of rubber for bicycle, and later motorcar tyres gave fresh impetus.

Around 1886, Edouard and André Michelin, grandsons of Barbier, one of the firm's founders, began to manufacture tyres. From then on, Clermont-Ferrand has been dominated by Michelin. A series of fortuitous events transformed an aristocratic old cathedral and university town into the bustling headquarters of the chubby and elastic Monsieur Bibendum.

It would be a mistake to read nostalgia into that last sentence. The reader should consult the majestic Arthur Young who visited Clermont in August 1789, and found it one of the *'worst built, dirtiest, and most stinking places I have met with.'*

Let a native defend it. Paul Bourget (1853-1935), poet, essayist and novelist, wrote, *'This is my town, the only one where I am not a stranger, a passer-by who can never return. My town, it is as much part of me as I am part of it'.* Clermont-Ferrand was a source of inspiration, too, to Maurice Barrès (1863-1923), the literary exponent of French nationalism, whose father came from Auvergne. Whether living writers feel the same passion towards the noisy, industrial city, I have yet to discover.

* * *

In art, the landscape of Auvergne has not inspired painters of high calibre. Three men, born at Le Puy during the last century, went elsewhere. Charles Cottet to Brittany; Charles Maurin, friend of Toulouse-Lautrec, to Montmartre; Albert Dubois-Pillet, the pointilliste who helped to found the *Salon des Indépendants* in 1884, and was the least well known of the founding group, stayed in Paris. Of present-day artists, Aristide Caillaud, the naive painter of Moulins, and Louis Neillot of Vichy, are known to specialist art collectors.

A much earlier native of Le Puy, Guy François (1570-1650) did work in the province, and his realistic religious pictures hang in churches at Le Puy, St. Bonnet, Pontgibaud and Gannat.

This leaves us with the masterpiece by the Master of Moulins, and his identity is in doubt. But more of this work — which, in any case, may have been painted by an artist from the Lowlands — in the next chapter.

Two musicians still enjoy more than just regional recognition. Andri Messager (1853-1929) from Montluçon, composed many elegant light operas, and for seven years was artistic director at Covent Garden. Emmanuel Chabrier (1841-94), born at Ambert, wrote orchestral works, and his 'España' was considered to be a *tour de force*.

A number of poets and novelists have drawn inspiration from the landscapes of their native Auvergne. The works of these *ecrivains du terroir* — lyrical or sentimental, elegaic or romantic — turn against the art of anguish, chaos of spirit, and over-civilisation, ushered in by Baudelaire. Their fame is correspondingly confined. In this category fall such writers as Pierre de Nolhac (1859-1936) of Ambert, and even Auvergne's most popular novelist and historian, Henri Pourrat (1887-1959), also of Ambert, whose strong regional flavour is illustrated in his epic *Gaspard des Montagnes* (1931). Also Arsène Vermenouze (1850 — 1910), born at Vielles near Aurillac, who wrote poetry in the *langue d'oc* and belonged to the Provençal revivalist tradition of the *félibre* movement animated by Frédéric Mistral.

An exception, perhaps, is Théodore de Banville (1823-91) of Moulins. A plaque marks his birthplace at 35 Rue de Bourgogne, and his statue stands in a square; de Banville's importance as a poet of France rather than of Auvergne lies in his rejection of the Romantic movement, favouring the classical structures of poetic expression and 'art for art's sake'. He belonged to the galaxy of 19th century poets known as the Parnassians.

The novelist who enjoyed the widest international reputation was Jules Romains. He was born Louis Farigoule in 1885 in the hamlet of Chapuze near the attractive village of St. Julien-Chapteuil in Velay. Prolific playwright, dramatic novelist and journalist, he developed an idealistic, nebulous and unconvincing notion called *unanimisme*. This he elaborated in some of his books as a concept of a superhuman spirit latent in every group, a collective soul. It appealed to some French writers such as Andre Gide, but English critics tend to dismiss it as insubstantial.

*　　*　　*

The story is told how a small boy of six, in 1887, left his home, a château near Clermont-Ferrand, with his younger sister. Against strict parental injunction, he was taking her for a long walk towards the hills before they were found. And what were they so disobediently up to? 'To see what is inside the volcanoes', answered the boy, prematurely indicating his future intellectual way of life.

The boy was Pierre Teilhard de Chardin (1881-1955) of whom the world at large knew nothing until after his death. Since then, the religious, philosophical and palaeontological writings of this scientific visionary have aroused universal interest and sometimes intense hostility.

Born in the little château — a *gentilhommière* or manor house, really — of Sarcenat outside Orcines, Teilhard came of a family proud of its lineage which could be traced back to the 14th century. It was proud of its traditions, its close family ties, its ultra-Catholic and feudal atmosphere in which mother radiated love and spiritual clarity, and father — a gentleman farmer — a certain intimidating reticence and intellectual interest in natural history, palaeography, and the history of Auvergne.

Teilhard's upbringing was strict; there was no concession to sentimentality or indulgence. How clearly this is reflected in the long, ascetic, muscular, responsive yet withdrawn face and far-seeing eyes. This childhood of bourgeois austerity was common to many families in the second half of the 19th century. He trained as a Jesuit. One of his teachers, Henri Brémond, remembered him as a very intelligent little Auvergnat, always first, almost excessively well behaved, and absorbed in a different world — the world of stones, in the reality of God in stones. Within the Jesuitical discipline, he trained as a geologist and palaeontologist, coming under the influence of a fellow Auvergnat, Marcellin Boulle (1861-1942). A stretcher-bearer in the 1914-18 War, Teilhard's bravery was admired by the troops he served at the front. Later, he taught at the Catholic Institute in Paris, and travelled to many parts of the world, though it is China, where his palaeological discoveries were made, with which he is mainly associated. He died suddenly in New York in 1955.

As long as Teilhard's researches were confined to the realm of science, his relations with his religious superiors were exemplary. But from 1926 on he began to enunciate theological ideas in connection with his science. He was ordered to devote himself to scientific researches only.

An outsider can only view with puzzled admiration the resolution in Teilhard of the conflict between total subservience to the authority of his Church, and the restless, enquiring spirit which drove the man to the important discoveries relating to the skulls of early man, and the wider conclusions he was to draw. For every aspect of his work — his movements abroad, his publications, his academic posts — he sought the permission of his seniors in Rome. He accepted their decisions without question. The inner distress they must have caused him, he never showed. For Teilhard there was no valid activity outside the Christian faith.

All his important books could be published only after his death, for the Jesuits had expressly forbidden their publication. His books were brought to the notice of the English-speaking world through Teilhard's friendship with

Sir Julian Huxley; paradoxical at first sight, this association of a scientist dedicated to the Absolute God with a scientific atheist dedicated to man. But Sir Julian understood the importance of Teilhard's interpretation of evolution, a vast process of becoming, of the expansion of human mental potential, the ultimate completion of human destiny.

Teilhard constructed a visionary's bridge between past and future, between static facts and the unity of evolution, between the scientifically measurable realities and the inner spirit and mystical vision of the Absolute.

At the heart of Matter
A heart of the World,
The heart of God.

This quotation heads one of his books. It enshrines a religious philosophy which many question, though no-one doubts his greatness as a scientist. What is this conviction that the stones of the geologist are the repository of the Spirit, that man is a prolongation of geology, that Spirit and thought envelop the earth, that they transform organisms in the processes of evolution, as bacteria do? For Teilhard, evolutionary life is being diversified, but is also converging towards a spiritual centre, the Ultra-personal God.

His language is sometimes hard to follow, for he had to invent new words to express new ideas; his assumptions are difficult to accept; his anguished optimism is not shared by all. But to judge by the Teilhard de Chardin societies that have sprung up the world over, his hopeful view of human destiny, his unification of matter and spirit, have touched a widely responsive chord. Father Pierre Teilhard de Chardin may have exerted more influence on world thought than any Auvergnat in the 2,000 years of the province's history.

11

BETWEEN THE LOIRE AND CHER

If you believe, as I do, that some roads merely shovel you to your destination in a peremptory sort of way, while others prepare your mind for it with tactful sympathy, then it is worth while searching out a road into Auvergne which does just this.

The fast and busy N7 slides smooth and straight along the broad valley of the Allier through Villeneuve-sur-Allier into Moulins. But the road which follows the *Canal latéral à la Loire* for many miles enters the very heart of an almost timeless France of towpaths and little humpback bridges, majestic rows of trembling poplars, old men whose lines would hate to be disturbed by a tug at the bait. It is a peaceful, simple and reflective journey with recurring images of Impressionist paintings. You can cross the Loire, coming from the north, at Gien, following first the wide river to Châtillon, then to track the Canal through small villages and a flat and somnolent landscape. Just before the coquettish village of Apremont, you leave the Canal and follow the Allier river. The first place of any size in Allier, along this road, is Le Veurdre, 123km from Gien.

It is the right introduction to the Bourbonnais.

On the road to Bourbon-l'Archambault and beyond, the wide harmony of the Bourbonnais horizons unfolds. Rich green pastures; creamy white and sleek Charollais cattle stand out with startling candle-like brilliance against the lush parkland grass; trees and hedgerows; strong farm buildings like those of neighbouring Burgundy; the occasional round tower; old men on bicycles, wearing pointed wooden clogs. It all looks content and prosperous; one could imagine man to be in his proper context with nature.

Even after a brief acquaintance with the rural parts of the Allier *département,* it becomes easy to see why 18th century English travellers spoke so well of this part of France. Laurence Sterne comes to mind. In his subtle, very modern, plotless, ironic *A Sentimental Journey through France and Italy*, first published in 1768, he called the Bourbonnois (as it was then spelled) the sweetest part of France which at vintage time filled him with 'the distress of plenty' — a telling phrase.

Just over twenty years later, a far more hardheaded judge who looked at the land with the eye of a farmer concerned with productivity and profit — Arthur Young — passed the same way and echoed Sterne. He found the Bourbonnais 'one of the finest provinces in France'.

*   *   *

It was close to Moulines, as Sterne spelled it, that one of his vague and chaste adventures befell him. This time it was with the poor, disordered Marie whom he found beneath a poplar tree — an incident he had already published in *Tristram Shandy*.

Moulins, for all its 27,500 population and streets a riotous mob of traffic, is a town of instant appeal. The eye is delighted with the variety of front elevations along the streets; the old façades are clean and well preserved. Cours Anatole France is a broad, tree-shaded boulevard which, with the Cours Jean Jaurès partly encircles the old town, for they were constructed on the ditch below the one-time defence walls. There are other wide, plane-shaded avenues which lend dignity and a sense of space to the administrative capital of the *département*.

From the 14th century Moulins rose from village obscurity to be the city-residence of the Bourbon dukes — who were to give France eight kings — and capital of the duchy at the end of the 15th century. Here, Duke Pierre II, husband of Anne, daughter of Louis XI, established a centre of art which drew musicians, painters and sculptors whose delicate style suggests a late flowering of medieval art. A short-lived artistic prosperity and political independence, however; for in 1523 Charles de Bourbon was found guilty of treason. The duchy was confiscated and absorbed by the Crown of France in 1561.

At the heart of the old city is the cathedral of Notre Dame, externally a mixture of Flamboyant Gothic and a 19th century imitation of 13th century Gothic. Within, twelve 15th and 16th century stained glass windows by specialists from Lyon are both beautiful and a record of some historical persons.

The masterpiece is in the sacristy. It is the triptych by the Master of Moulins, painted just before 1500. Who was the Master of Moulins? Of four candidates, experts seem to prefer one Jean Hey. When the outer wooden panels are closed, one sees an elegant Annunciation in grisaille. Opened, the panels reveal portraits of the donors of the triptych, Duke Pierre II of Bourbon and his masterful wife, Duchess Anne de Beaujeu and her daughter, kneeling, and being presented to the Virgin and Child in the central panel, by St. Peter and Ste. Anne.

The colours are sumptuous and clear; the whole is balanced and refined. Yet — and I speak only for myself— it is formal, worldly, unspiritual. The Virgin is a fleshy, pretty face; the Child is any pleasant, pot-bellied infant; the angels could have been posed by a bunch of pretty schoolgirls. When it comes to the patrons, the Master of Moulins does a smooth public relations exercise in 15th century paint, flattering his powerful and aristocratic patrons. Gone is the doubt, torment and spiritual passion and misery that had made medieval art so moving; extraverted realism has shown the Master of Moulins that salvation and the main chance are in the here and now.

Within the boulevards, the old town of narrow streets and houses of stone and red and black brickwork in lozenge formation, calls the stroller. Rue d'Allier has best preserved the 15th and 16th century buildings. South of the cathedral is the Jacquemart, or Jack-o'-the-clock, a belfry with an upper gallery, above which is the bell tower. Originally erected in the 15th century, the Jacquemart was partly burned down two hundred years later, and again in 1646, although it had not been in use for a long time until 1932. The hours are struck on the big bell, put up by Anne of Austria in 1956, by father Jacquemart in his 18th century grenadier's uniform, and by his wife, Jacquette. Their children strike the quarter hours on two little bells hung in 1658.

An interest in local ethnology will be satisfied in the Musée du Folklore et du Vieux Moulins, near the Jacquemart and Hôtel de Ville. There is a good collection of historical costumes. Two rooms are filled with illustrations of windmills from all over the world, a reminder that in the 13th century, there were windmills all along the banks of the Allier; from them the city took its name. In the Renaissance building of the Pavillon d'Anne de Beaujeu is housed the art and archaeology museum; the Musée Historique du Bourbonnais reviews the region's history, and is in the suburb of Yzeure, once the parent town of Moulins.

*   *   *

Reminders of the Bourbon past are to be found outside Moulins as well. Hilly Bourbon-l'Archambault, on the river Burge, has a lake, a ruined castle, a 12th century church, and a museum in which the past life of the Bourbonnais is recreated — quite apart from the town's main function of treating rheumatism. The hyphenation derives, first, from the Gaulish divinity, Borvo, who was the Gallic equivalent to classical Apollo, and who through his association with thermal waters was held to have the power of driving away disease. Borvo (sometimes Bormo) in Celtic denotes 'seething water', and his female companion was Damona, 'the Divine Cow'. The second part of the spa's name was bequeathed by Archambault I, seigneur of Bourbon. In 1283 Beatrix de Bourbon married the sixth son of St. Louis, Robert de Clermont, so that through this union the Bourbon kings who ruled France from Henri IV on, stemmed. When Moulins was made capital of the duchy of Bourbonnais in the 15th century, the little town of Bourbon would have fallen into oblivion but for the reputation of its waters. They drew the nobility, including the extrava-

Le Jacquemart, Moulins

gant Henrietta Maria (1609-69), wife of Charles I of England. The Revolution temporarily put an end to such ostentation; the castle was destroyed, and the spa's royal associations were to be obliterated by it being renamed Burge-les-Bains.

Between Moulins and Bourbon-l'Archambault are churches, some obscure, others well known. St. Menoux village is grouped round a lovely 12th century church, all that remains of a Benedictine abbey built two centuries earlier in memory of the Breton Menulphus who died here in the 7th century. A sarcophagus behind the altar contains the remains of St. Menoux.

Just north, the smaller village of Agonges also has a 12th century church with ancient ironwork on its doors, and 15th century frescoes in the sacristy. There are other delightful villages. Autry-Issards, Meillers, Besson, St. Hilaire on the edge of the Forêt de Grosbois in which are hidden ruins of old chapels and a priory; Gipcy, Marigny, Coulandon, and the ruins of the priory of St. Maurice near Autry-Issards, not even marked on the Michelin map.

By contrast, Souvigny is much visited. Set in rich agricultural country, and

The Church at Souvigny

known for its glassworks, Souvigny is regarded as having the finest ecclesiastical buildings in the Bourbonnais. They lie to one side, away from the main street which has a somewhat mournful appearance and is noisy with heavy lorries going to Moulins. The priory church of St. Pierre stands on rising ground, and was built on the site of an earlier church dedicated to St. Peter. The lands round Souvigny were owned by Aimard or Adhémar, an ancestor of the Bourbons. He ceded the property to the monks of Cluny in 915. The main parts of the massive buildings were erected in the 11th and 12th centuries, and there are similarities between them and those at Cluny itself.

Although the Cluniac monks brought fame to Souvigny, the priory had fallen into disrepair by the 15th century. Major alterations were ordered by the Bourbon dukes so that the church should become the family's burial place; their tombs are among the chief sights. The cloisters and sacristy were added in the 18th century. From the latter the little museum is reached. Its chief pride is a unique octagonal pillar of stone, carved early in the 12th century, though now only the upper half remains. On it are clearly seen, in carved medallions, the months and their zodiacal signs, and the labours of each month, harvesting in August; grape-picking in September; the acorn harvest in October; tilling in November; the collecting of the winter foods in December. Fabled beasts and weird faces alternate with other decorations.

*   *   *

East of Moulins is the Besbre valley which runs into the Loire. The valley is frequented mainly by fishermen; the little tributaries are trout-filled. Numerous Bourbonnais châteaux stand on the low hills. Following N480 downstream from Lapalisse, which itself has a *son-et-lumière* château, there appears next the 18th century château of Gléné (not marked on Michelin map 73); then Cindré to the left of the road, and Puyfol; to the right is ruined 13th century Chavroches. On the opposite side of the valley is the perfectly preserved 13th century Vieux-Chambord. Jaligny is a handsome Renaissance château; this is the village which holds a poultry market each Wednesday. Beauvoir, by the roadside, is a 15th century reconstruction. Toury, outside St. Pourçain-sur-Besbre, is a 15th century pink granite fortress.

To both left and right of the main road are paths leading to non-tourist villages. The west side is flat, and has innumerable pools, the southern outposts of the marshes of Sologne Bourbonnais. On the other side of N480 is a little segment — between Dompierre-sur-Besbre, Le Donjon and Digoin — about which guide books have little to say. Explorers of the unfamiliar will not find anything very spectacular, but at Molinet, for instance, they will come upon 14th century murals in St. Pierre-aux-liens; at Neuilly-en-Donjon, the tympan of the church represents the Adoration of the Magi and angels sounding trumpets. The Kings are mounted on very oriental looking beasts, and very precariously at that. The carved area is crowded with ungainly yet expressive 12th century figures.

Between Le Donjon and Lapalisse a spur of hills rises over 500m, and for a panorama of the whole Besbre valley, the viewpoint is Puy St. Ambroise (442m), 11km from Jaligny.

*   *   *

The road south from Moulins is the straight and often congested N9 which follows the hilly left bank of the Allier. It is the quickest way to St. Pourçain-sur-Sioule, 31km away. Smaller by far than Moulins, St. Pourçain gives the same initial impression of architectural attractiveness. It was named after the slave Portianus who miraculously saved Auvergne from the ravages of Thierry, son of Clovis, and founded a Benedictine abbey at St. Pourçain in the 6th century. The chief architectural sight is the one-time abbey of St. Croix, a curious jumble of shapes and periods.

St. Pourçain is a popular centre, and the wine of which it is so proud is eminently drinkable. One place to go to is Verneuil-en-Bourbonnais, a still medieval village; another is Saulcet nearby, to look at the church murals. At Montaigu-le-Blin is a 13th century castle, and Billy has another of the same period on its hill top, and is reached from the Forêt de Sarcenat.

Southwest of St. Pourçain is the Sioule valley. N9 follows it, but the lesser roads are far more attractive and meander to villages, some of which have restaurants with a reputation. Chantelle is one of them. It, too, has associations with the Bourbons who constructed a fortress in the 11th century, part of which was converted into a country house at which Pierre II and Anne de Beaujeu spent spare time away from Moulins. Now only two ruined towers remain, but there are some picturesque old houses in the village, and the view of the river Bouble's deep ravine is striking.

At Ussel-d'Allier, not far away, in the restored Renaissance *gentilhommière* of Château de la Croisette is an art collection which is open to the public in summer, and has works by Braque, Chagall, Matisse, Picasso and other modern masters, as well as Aubusson tapestries and Limoges enamelware.

Jenzat is another village that pleases the eye; its church contains distempered murals painted in the 15th century in a realistic and naive style by an unknown artist who goes by the name 'Master of Jenzat'.

Or Chouvigny — with a château, of course — at the entrance to gorges of the same name. Or Pont de Menat with its old humpback bridge. Or Ebreuil whose church of St. Léger is one of the best examples of Auvergnat Romanesque; the porch, statuary and frescoes are outstanding 12th century works. Charroux, Bellenaves and Château de-Rochefort are all worth searching out. Near the latter is the Rouzat viaduct, one of the large, light metal bridges built by Alexandre Gustave Eiffel, a pioneer in air-resisting bridge building. This viaduct was erected in 1869, thirteen years before Eiffel tackled the great Garabit viaduct in Cantal, and nearly twenty years before he put up his masterpiece, the Eiffel Tower in Paris.

*   *   *

There is no need for Vichy to delay us again. The spa, its agreeable parks, as well as the one at Bellerive, and a museum or two almost exhaust Vichy's sightseeing possibilities, but not the excursions. Old Cusset still has some charming gabled houses in its centre. The Bourbon Château de Busset; the view over the Allier river and the distant hills from the Site des Hurlevants; the view from the 12th century church at Cognat — all these are excursions at no distance from Vichy.

One of the most attractive roads out of Vichy is N495 which follows the Sichon valley upstream, so rising steadily towards the Bois Noirs and Monts de la Madeleine. After about twenty km along the road, a turning to the left leads quickly to the hamlet of Glozel. It boasts a hut which is a museum calling itself Musée Préhistorique. The story behind it will appeal to anyone whose archaeological bent is laced with a taste for unresolved riddles, academic disputes and a bit of skulduggery.

In 1924, some apparently remarkable artifacts of pottery, terracotta objects, bone fragments and inscribed pebbles were unearthed down in the valley of the Vareille stream close to Glozel, on a plot of ground known as the Champs des Morts, by a family named Fradin. The finds created a stir. To some experts, the inscribed stones were unique and undeciphered, which led them to propound new theories about the origin of language and writing. By 1927, most prehistorians concluded that the artifacts were modern fakes. There the matter would have rested, a curio of both archaeology and psychology, rather in the manner of our own Sussex 'Piltdown Man'. Nothing in the intervening years has turned up in the region to link its culture with the Glozelian, a highly suspicious circumstance to the prehistorians. More recently, though, thermoluminescent analysis has suggested that, after all, the items were prehistoric, dating them between 700 B.C. and 200 A.D. Professor Glyn Daniel puts the matter in clear perspective in a letter. What we now know, he says, is that there is something wrong with these scientific techniques. Scientists are confused, and the dispute is no longer between archaeology and science but within science itself. The credibility of all thermoluminescent dating is now at stake, for other techniques of dating contradict the TL method.

Clearly, the artifacts are fakes, but there they are, respectably on show for a fee, every day, while the Champ des Morts, wired off, can still be reached by a steep path from the hamlet.

Continuing on N495, the next village is Ferrières-sur-Sichon in the Montagne Bourbonnaise, the first intimation of more mountainous country bey-

ond. To its north is Châtel-Montagne surrounded by wooded slopes of the Bois de l'Assise with pastureland, cultivated fields and ridges reaching 1,000m in the Monts de la Madeleine, the barrier between Auvergne and the Lyonnais hills on the further side of the Loire valley. South of Ferrières is the high, pine covered plateau of the Bois Noirs. Its highest point is Puy de Montocel at 1,287m, where the *départements* of Allier, Loire and Puy-de-Dôme meet.

*   *   *

So far, this chapter has visited the eastern half of Allier. The main way into it to the west is by the Bourges — Montluçon road, N144, through the Roman 'centre of France' at Bruère-Allichamps, mentioned early in Chapter 1. A number of lesser roads from the north enter Allier through the Forêt de Tronçais, the finest oak and beech forest in France, and a rival to any other in Europe. It is, understandably, a popular holiday region, for there are walks, camping and picnic sites, lakes for swimming, sailing and fishing, as well as mammalian and bird life. St. Bonnet-Tronçais is a delightful village in the heart of the forest; other small resort towns stand at the perimeter, such as Urcay, Meaulne and Cérilly.

The system of forestry practised in Forêt de Tronçais was laid down by Louis XIV's great minister Colbert, 300 years ago, although the forest has had a chequered career both before and after Colbert. Neglect and over-exploitation have plagued it, and it is only since 1835 that a proper rhythm of forestry has been applied in the way Colbert had instructed, based on the economically advantageous life span of oak trees, estimated at 220 years (much less for beeches, of course).

For the ecologist, the Forêt de Tronçais is sited on poor but wholesome soil which, retarding the trees' rate of growth, produces their very high quality. Frosts can occur as late as mid-May in this 'continental' climate area. They toughen the timber and check coarse growth in older oaks, even if they tend to split younger ones. Spring rain is plentiful. Owing to past abuse, parts of the forest were considered unsuited to oak, and Scots pines were planted. They helped to fix the nitrates in the humus, allowing oaks gradually to be reintroduced. In this forest, the first experiments in crossing sessile and pedunculate oaks took place, from which four hybrids resulted.

Meaulne lies at the western margin of the forest. The name will sound a sympathetic chord among admirers of that strange, half-dream, excessively nostalgic novel, *Le Grand Meaulnes* by Alain-Fournier, a lament for lost youth, written in 1913 before the author died in the trenches at the age of 27.

Just below Meaulne, the river Aumance joins the Cher. D157 follows the

The Château, St. Yorre

Hérrison, Allier

quiet, pleasant valley, past Châteaux Le Creux and La Roche. There are few hamlets until you come to Châteloy, whose church has some over-restored 13th century murals. Then the charming village of Hérisson, a cluster of old roofs snuggling round the ruins of a 13th century fortress. Harpignies (1819-1916) painted many of his best landscapes — particularly the Saut du Loup — in the vicinity. A few 15th and 16th century houses survive, chief among them the *gendarmerie* and the so-called synagogue.

Anyone with the patience to penetrate to the heart of old Montluçon through the northern industrial clutter, will come upon a 15th century church built by Louis II de Bourbon, and a castle put up by him, now housing the city's museums: folklore, historical, archaeological, natural history and pottery sections. A whole section is devoted to the history of the *vielle*, the hurdy-gurdy about which I wrote earlier in connection with the Bourbonnais-Auvergnat dance, the *bourrée*.

Seven km. from Montluçon lies Néris-les-Bains on the edge of the Combrailles plateau, and surrounded by woodlands. Néris came our way in the chapter on spas. It is a pleasant little place to visit even in a state of perfect health. Quiet, dignified, enjoying an equable summer climate, its antiquities repay the excursion.

A sacred place of healing for the Gauls, it was presided over by the god Neriomagus. With the arrival of the Romans it became *Aquae Nerii*. They constructed the baths, amphitheatre, temples, villas and aqueducts; it was a large and thriving town. The three Roman baths can be seen in Parc des Chaudes. In Parc des Arènes are the remnants of the Roman amphitheatre which had been constructed in the flank of a valley. At 26 Rue Boistrot-Desserviers, near the casino, the local archaeological society has put on a display of things excavated from the Roman sites. To the left of the entrance to the Grand Etablissement in the same street is Musée Rieckötter where marble columns, capitals, pottery, bronzes, coins, jewels, medals from prehistoric and Roman times can be seen. Within the picturesque Romanesque church are vestiges of a little Christian basilica of the 4th to 6th centuries. Next to the church is a Merovingian necropolis of the 6th century whose sarcophagi, constructed out of earlier Roman debris, contained skeletons when they were found in 1966. All the heads were facing east, towards 'the land of Christ', as was customary in those times.

A small triangle of the Allier *département* obtrudes west of the river Cher, on both sides of the Montluçon — Culan road (N143), where little hills and valleys hide occasional and not much publicised châteaux or old churches. For instance, Domérat has an 11th century crypt. Huriel, the most interesting village, has a handsome 12th century church whose baptismal font is covered with crudely carved reptiles and a dove. There are also remains of a castle, and the large village square has — unusual sight — a cedar tree in it.

12

PUY-DE-DÔME

Not far south of Vichy the river Allier is joined by the Dore, just in Puy-de-Dôme. N106 follows the Dore valley to its source beyond Arlanc in the Monts du Livradois, and an attractive subalpine run it becomes. Not immediately; St. Yorre is a nondescript prolongation of Vichy, and specialises in bottling mineral waters.

Today's N106 follows fairly closely a prehistoric track. Originally used by Gallic tribes, it was improved and paved by the Romans (a section is visible near Villefort in Lozère), and called *Via Rigordana*, the Roman road from Nîmes, through the Cévennes, to the north. It was the sole route from Languedoc to Auvergne until the end of the Middle Ages. It was used by pilgrims and traders; by Protestant preachers and, since Neolithic times, by shepherds taking their flocks to high summer pastures in Lozère and the Aubrac mountains.

The first digression from this venerable road should be the left turn at Ris-Gare, through Ris with an early 11th century church, all that remains of a priory founded in 978. A little way on in this vine- and tree-filled valley is Châteldon. The good townspeople have left the memorial to Pierre Laval standing, for, whatever verdict history has passed on him, they must believe he had served his birthplace honourably. Châteldon is a delight: its setting in the green valley of the Vauziron which flows gently about the village; the square and streets with timbered, arcaded and balconied houses of 15th and 16th century vintners; its 14th century clock tower; an astronomical clock made by a master carpenter in the last century; the church's 16th century primitive painting of the Crucifixion. They hold a wine festival on the third Monday of October.

Thiers, on the main road again, sits with panache above the Durolle gorge; the river contains properties suited to the paper and cutlery industries that made Thiers wealthy. Every so often, the steep and winding streets open a sudden prospect of gleaming buildings on the hillside and vistas beyond.

Gregory of Tours in 531 mentions Thiers as *Tigernum Castrum*, but its rise to fame dates from the First Crusade (1096-99) when the techniques of tempered steel were brought back from Palestine by Auvergnat Crusaders. Paper-making has died out, but steel-making has flourished ever since. Old Thiers by the river is intriguing. From the 15th century on, artisans in tiny workshops used the water for their grindstones, and half-timbered houses line the lanes descending to the river. Some are decorated with wood carvings; some have tiny gardens, Especially interesting are Rue de la Coutellerie, and Rue du Bourg which leads to the carefully restored 15th century building, Le Pirou. The old wooden workshops along the Durolle valley are deserted and falling down, but you can still see the innumerable channels, dams and waterfalls that provided water-power in the past. The modern steel factories are higher up, away from the town centre.

Musée Fontenille-Mondière should dispel romantic illusions about artisanal work in the past. It shows how arduous and cold it could be when men lay prone for hours operating grindstones inches above the Durolle. George Sand described her visit to the steel workshops in *La Ville Noire* (1861).

Between Châteldon, Thiers and the boundary with the Loire *département*, the Bois Noirs offer a variety of hilly roads leading to pleasant villages, some of them also cutlery cottage industry villages.

It may sound a little dismissive to say that the most interesting thing about Ambert is an excursion away from it. But there is little doubt that Moulin Richard-de-Bas, four km east, along the Val de Laga, is fascinating. This working museum traces the history of paper-making from the year A.D. 105 when the Chinese invented it, and how it was brought to Europe by the Arabs. A medieval craftsman's living quarters have been reproduced. You can watch high quality paper being made on wooden presses and passed through vats which have scarcely changed since the 14th century. In a little garden are grown plants used in the manufacture and decoration of paper. Finished sheets can be bought. For centuries, the whole Laga valley, along with Ambert's 300 mills, produced much of the paper needed in France.

*   *   *

Clermont-Ferrand stands physically in the centre of Puy-de-Dôme; it is the axis from which the political, intellectual and commercial history of Auvergne has radiated. It may not be everyone's idea of a touring base, for it is a commercial and industrial city, but it has advantages.

Boulevards encircle the shopping and business sections, the majority of tourist hotels, the remains of the old town, and the active and helpful Offices du Tourisme, one at 69 Boulevard Gergovia, the other in Place de Jaude. Montferrand, until 1731 a separate, rival town, is predominantly industrial, and is severed by N9 — the road to Spain — with hoardings, patrol stations, factory frontages, incessant traffic — the unacceptable face of urbanism — but at least the through-routes avoiding Clermont are unambiguously marked.

Thiers, the Durolle

The residential suburbs of Chamalières, Durtol, and the fashionable spa of Royat, lie on the westwards heights.

East of N106, between Thiers and Ambert, are the Monts du Forez. Again, narrow, winding roads pass first through oaks and chestnuts, rising to the beech and birch belt, and to the pinewoods where the woodcutters work. Thinly populated, here are space and solitude, and villages with ruined castles and splendid views. And there are the cols over the watershed, such as Col du Béal, at 1,390m, turning its ideas towards winter sports. Nearer the Thiers-

118

Ambert road are flourishing little tourist resorts: Vertolaye, Job and the Volpie waterfall, and Valcivières.

Courpière comes after Thiers; some of the half-timbered houses surrounding the church are reminiscent of Thiers. Sixteen km further on is the prettiest little town along this road, Olliergues. It is daintily announced by a grey-roofed little spire and openwork clock-tower above red roofs and iron-brown walls, some of which stand sheer over the Dore river.

On approaching Ambert, the valley broadens out to the plain of Ambert, a depression below the plateau of the Livradois to the west, an area of quiet charm, of woods interspersed with fields and open country in the higher parts, and cultivated plots lower down.

Ambert

As far as Billom (which has some medieval houses in Rue des Boucheries) on this side of the Dore are châteaux in profusion. Some can be visited: St. Dierd'Auvergne; Les Martinanches; Ravel; and Aulteribe, well known for its period furniture, Flanders tapestries and paintings in the much-restored 15th century château. Others are ruined; some well placed on hilltops, like Mauzon which is quite a walk up from the village, a massive triple-walled fortress with nineteen towers, started in the 12th century on the site of an ancient stronghold, *Mandanum*. Others are coyly hidden by copses.

Place de Jaude is at the heart of Clermont. Round about are shops, cafés and bus termini. It is planted out with handsome catalpa trees whose large yellow-green leaves and trumpet-like flowers impart an exotic and vernal touch in summer. It is said that they are the only trees able to tolerate the carbonate of lime which filters through the soil from the petrified fountains of St. Alyre, a little to the north. In the square are the equestrian statue of Vercingetorix, and the monument to General Desaix, of Marengo fame.

Old Clermont is northwest of the Place de Jaude. 16th to 18th century mansions are grouped about the cathedral, a northern Gothic building, unique in that it is the only cathedral to have been constructed of Volvic lava; a massive, deep-grey and slightly chilling edifice. On this site, a basilica had been erected in the 5th century by bishop Namatius. It was burned down in 761, rebuilt, destroyed by Normans in 915; then a Carolingian church whose vestiges can be seen in the crypt. Interior proportions achieve lightness through the use of hard-grained Volvic stone; slender columns and vaults could be created without the building crashing down. The stained glass windows are sumptuous, especially those in the side chapels. They were made in the 13th century in the workshop which made the windows for La Sainte-Chapelle in Paris. Early sarcophagi, carvings, frescoes of different periods, a complicated Jack-o'-the-clock (stolen from Issoire in the 16th century), are among the cathedral's contents.

Clermont's principal monument is the 11th and 12th century basilica of Notre Dame du Port, built somewhat later than most of the other large Romanesque churches in Auvergne. Revolutionaries defaced some parts, and 19th century restoration others, but this is Auvergnat architecture at its most impressive, particularly the chevet and its cluster of four apsidal chapels. They are decorated with the characteristic bands of multi-coloured mosaic stone. The walls were built with mortared blocks of lava; the supports, arcades and frameworks to the bays with coarse-grained yellowish stone called arkose.

Inside, the capitals of the choir are among the best stone-carvings in Auvergne; this series of religious stories can be illuminated — and needs to be.

A whole section of old Montferrand survives and has undergone restoration. They are the *hôtels* or mansions, dating from Gothic and Renaissance periods. The oldest is Maison de l'Eléphant, 12 Rue Kléber, a 13th century house so named from the traces of a fresco representing an elephant on a first-floor wall. Restoration has brought to light carvings in stone and wood, and fine spiral staircases. Well over a dozen of these buildings, with their courtyards, galleries, columns and turrets, give a vivid impression of how a town looked all those centuries ago.

Of excursions close at hand, the one to the Puy-de-Dôme is foremost. You can motor up to it (the last part is a toll road), or you can walk up the steep path from Col de Ceyssat, on the path the Romans used to carry up the materials for the great temple of Mercury. The temple ruins are now mere fragments, but the building must have been enormous and magnificent. Marbles were brought from afar; a colossal bronze statue of Mercury was laboured at for ten years by the Greek sculptor, Zenodorus. The panorama is the chief draw. You look upon the volcanic chains, and far beyond. With clear visibility, your sight commands eleven *départements*, an eighth of France.

In the opposite direction is the Plateau de Gergovie, an elevated plain at 734m, edged by steep escarpments, where, in 53 B.C. Caesar's army received a temporary reverse at the hands of Vercingetorix. A commemorative monument to the Gaulish warrior, 26m high, made of Volvic stone, was put up in 1900; there is a little site museum as well.

* * *

North of Clermont is the sizeable town of Riom whose core consists of dignified grey stone façades of buildings erected between the 15th and 17th centuries. They are the mansions of lawyers and judges, when Riom was the seat of Auvergne's judiciary.

That once proud mantle was to fall shabbily on Riom's shoulders in 1942, when a group of politicians and soldiers — Blum, Daladier, Reynaud and Gamelin — were put on trial by the Vichy government which hoped to pin the guilt for the French collapse in 1940 on them. So skilfully did the defendants turn trial into debate, and so cast discredit on Pétain and the General Staff, that the charges were quietly dropped.

The old buildings are full of reticent charm and architectural variety. In addition, there are 17th and 18th century fountains. Musée Régional d'Auvergne, an ethnology museum, brings the region's day-to-day past back to life. Musée Mandet's art gallery has exhibits of various European schools and periods down to the present day; there are works by Frans Hals, Watteau, Titian. Eglise Notre Dame du Marthuret contains a 12th century Black Virgin, and a charming statue of the 'Virgin with the Bird'; it is the Infant Jesus who is playing with a bird. It is probably 14th century, from the period when the Duc de Berry attracted artists to his château-court at Riom, where the Palais de Justice now stands. In the Hôtel de Ville is the Joan of Arc Museum which contains the letter the Maid wrote to the Riomois in 1429, appealing for help in the struggle against the English.

Mozac is virtually a western suburb of Riom. Its venerable abbey, founded in 681 by St. Calmin, was once one of the major abbeys of France. The first to begin its slow destruction were the Huguenots in 1592; now, the external remains are ugly. Inside, the 12th century capital carvings are among the loveliest in Auvergne. There is a profusion of themes: from the second Woman at the Tomb of Christ, guarded by soldiers in 12th century military apparel, to Jonah being swallowed and ejected by the whale; from acanthus leaves, human masks, eagles, griffons, centaurs, to winged and kneeling angels.

A casket of Limousin enamel-work contains the remains of St. Calmin. Another rare, painted casket holds the relics of St. Austremoine who preached the Gospel in Auvergne, in the treasury. The sacristy is where the seal with which King Pépin the Short authenticated the relics of St. Austremoine — for he had himself carried on his shoulders the mortal remains of the saint from Volvic — can be seen.

Three km away from Riom is Marsat's Romanesque church; in it is the celebrated 12th century Black Virgin which was referred to in Chapter 8. Châtelguyon spa, the Gorges d'Enval, the romantic Château de Tournoël, and Châteaugay, whose castle keep and long-distance views vie with the equally famous vineyards at its sloping feet; are all within a short radius of Riom.

Between the castles of Tournoël and Châteaugay is Volvic, whose name has been reiterated whenever the buildings of the region have been mentioned. It stands on its *cheire* or hardened lava stream from the Nugère volcano. Here they quarry the black lava out of which so much of Auvergne has been built, as well as — for fifty years — Michelin road signs and telegraph posts throughout France, to say nothing of the gloomy cemetery at Volvic itself.

*   *   *

Flanking the west side of the Monts Dômes are the Combrailles, a series of undulating, rising plateaux, between the Bourbonnais and the approaches to the upper Dordogne. Their ancient Permian granite gives open country of wide, wooded valleys, dotted with irregularly shaped lakes, reed-lined and shallow, on the border with Creuse. Largest of them is the somewhat mournful Etang de Chancelade, whose surface of 360 acres covers water no more than four metres deep.

The entry from Allier into Puy-de-Dôme through the Gorges de Chouvigny belies this description. The road from Ebreuil follows the north bank of the fast-flowing Sioule, passes St. Gal's water mill, and the recently restored Château de Chouvigny. The castle's history goes back to the 13th century, when it must have looked down on the medieval pilgrims fording the river on their way to Compostella.

The road slices its way into the gorge, and gives striking views of concave and convex rocks which meanders in the river have eaten out. With Château-

Orcival, Puy de Dôme

neuf-les-Bains the road has emerged from the gorges into a spa treating arthritis, where a series of hamlets dot each side of the Sioule, granite on the left, porphyry on the right.

No road now follows the Sioule and you have to make a detour through St. Gervais-d'Auvergne to reach it again at the highest railway bridge in France, the Viaduc des Fades, built early this century.

A delightful run southwards in the Sioule valley brings you to the romantic site of ruined 13th century Chartreuse de Port-Ste. Marie, some of whose Renaissance wood panels have been preserved in the church at Manzat, 16 km away. Here, you are right at the edge of the Combrailles. At no great distance from Manzat is the almost circular volcanic crater-lake of fish-stocked Gour de Tazenat, marking the northern limit of the Monts Dômes. It is surrounded by steep and mostly wooded cliffs whose green is reflected in the clear, still waters of this deep lake, in total contrast with Etang de Chancelade, with which this survey of the Combrailles began.

* * *

The really popular holiday region of Auvergne may be said to begin south of Clermont-Ferrand. A diversity of scenery, the freshness of subalpine altitudes, villages and towns whose attractive architecture is ready-made for tourism, and four or five of the most impressive Romanesque churches. Once the sophistications of Clermont's golf course, and the eight km *Circuit automobile d'Auvergne* where the annual Auvergne trophies are raced for at the end of June, have been left behind, you are in the Monts Domes.

Lac d'Aydat, at 825m, is a deep crater-lake, surrounded by pine woods, forest tracks and holiday homes. Further on, Murol, overwhelmed by its huge castle, is a holiday centre on the Couze de Chambon. Lac Chambon nearby is shallow and island dotted. A little to the west is St. Nectaire, combining the functions of summer resort and thermal station at St. Nectaire-le-Bas, and a place of pilgrimage for lovers of 12th century architecture at St. Nectaire-le-Haut. Unlike some other famous Auvergnat churches, this massive church sits on a hilltop; you can inspect it from all points of the compass.

Another approach is by Vic-le-Comte. Among its old streets is a Sainte-Chapelle, built to house a Thorn of the Cross by a descendant of the Scottish royal family, John Stuart, in 1501. He had become Count of Auvergne through marriage. You pass ruined Château de Buron, perched on a basalt *dyke*, and make for the busy engineering town of Issoire whose church of St. Austremoine is another handsome Romanesque edifice. Again, the capitals here are

Roche Tuilière, Puy de Dôme

wonderful examples of that mixture of vision and down-to-earth realism, of skill and simplicity, in the art of 12th century sculptors. These carvings suffered at the hands of the notorious Captain Merle who ravaged for the Calvinist cause, in 1575; he tried to bring the whole building down by sawing through a support-pillar, but nothing happened. 19th century restoration hardly helped; it was responsible for the revolting interior paintwork.

From Issoire there is a tantalising choice of routes westwards. The answer is to find time to make a circular tour. On the northern road is Champeix surrounded by vine-slopes, and Montaigut-le-Blanc (why white?) — castle above, village beneath, terraced gardens in a curve to the Couze below. Both extend a welcoming atmosphere. And so to St. Nectaire.

Or by the Pavin valley along N496, sometimes an open, sometimes an enclosed route. 14th century murals on the ruined walls of the castle at St. Floret. 15th century murals in the church at Chastel. Then the Grottes de Jonas, caves scooped out by the hand of early man, and enlarged in medieval times; some local antiquities are on show.

Besse-en-Chandesse, at 1,050m, smells of tangy mountain air and pasturelands. Sober 15th and 16th century houses and shops of dark lava stone are lightened by quaint shapes, turrets and steep grey roofs. Besse is a pleasure to look on; it is also crowded in summer. Between Besse and Super-Besse, a recently developed winter sports centre, is the volcanic Lac Pavin (from the latin *pavens*, dreadful), high up, rock- and tree-lined. It is overlooked by Puy de Montchal from whose summit are extensive views.

A third route south leads through Orcival; another great Auvergnat Romanesque church, in the wooded valley of the Sioulet. Many people argue that it has the finest proportions, majesty and austerity of all Auvergne churches. 400 years after it was built, an earth tremor necessitated rebuilding parts of it; the Revolutionaries knocked down the spire which was reproduced (though shortened) in the 19th century. It, too, has fine sculptured capitals. Not least of interest is the 12th century Notre Dame d'Orcival, Auvergne's loveliest Virgin in Majesty.

Beyond Orcival, off D27, an uphill walk leads to La Roche Branladoire, an immense rock balancing on a natural fulcrum, so that a man can set the mass a-swinging.

The road rises between Roche Tuilière, an eroded volcanic stack on the right, and Roche Sanadoire, the relic of a cone, on the left. Over Col de Guéry (1,264m) and its lake, with a southward view of the Monts Dore and the high peak of Puy de Sancy (1,885m). From the spa of Le Mont-Dore you can get to the foot of Puy de Sancy; then a cable-car; finally the summit on foot.

Roche Sanadoire

Massif Central — La Route du Sancy

The eye is drawn towards the granite plateau of Artense to south and south-west, which stretches from the Rhue valley and Lac Chauvet in the east across to the Dordogne river in the west. The Dordogne has been dammed at Bort-les-Orgues (just in Corrèze), a mass of concrete walls and pipes and hydro-electrics. The reservoir it has formed is a beautiful lake, which has left the six turrets and elegant walls of Château du Val, floodlit in summer, stranded on a rock and joined by a causeway to the shore. Bort's other showpiece is the phonolithic basalt mass of 'organ pipes' outside the uninspiring town.

The Artense, once poor and marshy, now supports a few agreeable little holiday villages such as La Tour d'Auvergne, Condat, Egliseneuve-d'Entraigues. Over its wide pastures browse the deep brown Salers cattle, and much of St. Nectaire cheese is made in the district.

13

THE HORIZONS OF VELAY

In Haute-Loire, one kind of landscape imprints itself on the memory. It is the *planèze*, the high, undulating plateaux of the Monts de la Margeride and Monts du Velay, between 800m and 1,000m. The eye is carried across great distances towards peaks and ranges which rise only a few more hundred metres above the plateaux. Some people say that the clarity of Mediterranean light touches these wide horizons. But I find that the clarity has a strange, pearly quality I have not seen further south. A drive by the high main road from St. Flour to Le Puy illustrates forcibly that this landscape is clear, sober and remote. It comes down to earth, as it were, where the rivers Allier and Loire slice through the upland scenery.

To follow the upper Loire valley (with some digressions) through Haute-Loire provides as rich a diversity of scenery, places and history as one could wish for. The river enters the *département* near Aurec, and the narrow D47 plunges straight into the Loire gorges and out again to Monistrol-sur-Loire (actually nowhere near the river but on an attractive tributary).

The main N88 goes to industrial Yssingeaux, surrounded by volcanic peaks whose names are prefixed by *suc*, blister-like humps of once soft lava. Mont Meygal, at 1,436m surveys a strange volcanic landscape. Between Mont Meygal and Le Puy is St. Julien-Chapteuil on D15, a small town whose houses are roofed with grey *lauzes* slabs or tiles, where hand-made lace is still produced. This is where the writer Jules Romains spent his youth.

East of Yssingeaux, near the border with Ardeche, is the summer resort of Tence at the upper end of the Gorges du Lignon. More roofs of heavy slabs of phonolithic lava to hold off the winter storms, and not unlike our Horsham stone. Another little resort, mainly for children, is Chambon-sur-Lignon, upstream from Tence, and higher, with a fresher climate. Chambon is a Protestant centre, and has a Collège Cévenol of importance. Both the village and its setting have appeal.

Back to the Loire at Monistrol. A secondary road (D12) crosses the river to follow the gorges through Retournac whose Romanesque church catches the eye because it is of sandstone, and yellow, unlike the ubiquitous grey-black of so many buildings in this volcanic region. Then the contented looking village of Chamalières-sur-Loire (not to be confused with the suburb of Clermont-Ferrand), spread along the river bank. Its restored church — all that remains of a 10th century abbey — is the most attractive Romanesque building hereabouts. Finely proportioned inside and out, a 13th century mural of the Virgin in Majesty can be made out on a pillar near the high altar. In the unusually large apse is a beautifully carved stoup of four prophets, back to back. This came originally from the cloister by the river, now in ruins.

Hugging the bends in the river, the road turns south after Vorey to reach Lavoûte-sur-Loire and the fortress of Lavoûte-Polignac high above it. Set arrogantly on a bluff, with the river almost looping a circle at its base, the castle was built in the 13th century and rebuilt in the 17th. The first owner was the Bishop of Le Puy. He had it taken from him by the Polignac family who held it until its sale to the state during the Revolution. Recovered by the Polignacs in 1815, it was sold again in 1862. It was now in almost total ruin, but the determined Polignacs acquired it again twenty years later. It has been rebuilt. Visitors are shown over the place; there are tapestries, furnishings and archives, and, not least, portraits of generations of Polignacs by such distinguished painters as Rigaud, Largillière, Van Loo, David and Madame Vigée-Lebrun. In summer, there is son-et-lumière.

The original Polignac lair was a little distance away off the La Chaise-Dieu to Le Puy road at Polignac. Living in a world of medieval brigandage, the first Polignacs built a fortress on a massive block of rock. Little beside the restored keep remains. By the 17th century, the world had changed, and the Polignacs had given up infamy for diplomacy and respectability, and built the château at Lavoûte-Polignac. In the keep are some lapidary fragments, including a milestone bearing the Emperor Tiberius's name, from St. Paulien, and a so-called mask of Apollo. For the story goes that there had been on this spot a famous temple of Apollo, to which the Emperor Claudius came (he ruled between A.D. 41 and A.D. 54) in order to consult the oracle. But, as Peter Gorham comments, the huge mask on the first floor of the tower has a beard. Since when has Apollo — the embodiment of youth and athleticism — been depicted with a beard?

From Lavoûte-sur-Loire the river is hustled through the narrows of the Gorges de Peyredeyre. Le Puy-en-Velay is quickly reached, the Loire curving away to leave Le Puy on a tiny tributary.

Le Puy is one of those not-to-be-missed-on-any-account towns of the guidebooks. I cannot share the enthusiasm. I find it drab. The prospect from the surrounding hills is certainly striking — the cathedral of Notre Dame on its knoll; the two needles of lava bearing a chapel on one, a statue on the other.

Le Puy, Haute Loire

It is a town of some size — 29,500 inhabitants — and importance, the prefectorial town of Haute-Loire and seat of a bishopric. The cathedral can be described as 'impressive', 'imposing', or 'remarkable'. Its west front is the only part that can be seen properly (from Rue des Tables); the rest is hemmed in by the bishop's palace, cloisters and the old town. Sixty steps lead up to the west face, Auvergnat Romanesque in polychrome lava. Alternating bands of red, white and black stones surround each arch — I think there are thirty-three — and fill the blind arches. 'Zebra-like', Baring-Gould called it. Not a bad description. Still, it may be that the façade underwent major alterations in the 17th century.

The side chapel doors are of carved 13th century cedarwood. The interior is huge, plain and dark; the Arab influence is noticeable. Baring-Gould made cutting remarks about the Black Virgin which replaced the one burned by the Revolutionaries, observing that it was nevertheless better than the original. But the wooden figure is still venerated, just as the original had been since the pilgrimage to Compostella started, with Le Puy as an important halting-place.

In the treasury are some interesting items, including the Bible written by Theodulf early in the 9th century, the finest surviving example of Carolingian caligraphy. Even though the 'zebra-like' design is repeated in the cloister, it is the most delightful part of the cathedral. The capitals of the darkly volcanic columns are finely carved, and the 12th century railings there are wonderfully wrought.

Musée Crozatier is interesting for its examples of lace work. During the long winters in medieval times, the poorer women of Velay migrated to Le Puy, organising themselves into lacemaking 'congregations'. Until earlier this century, lacemaking had been the main industry of Haute-Loire which was, in fact, the most important lacemaking centre in the world. Yet all the material of linen tweed had to come from Holland, brought on foot over the execrable roads of Auvergne. Every village and hamlet had a *béate*, a woman who taught the children, ran the crèche, tended the sick, laid out the dead, and gave counsel to those who asked for it. She also taught the girls how to use the bobbins. Almost nothing of this picturesque and socially tightly-knit cottage industry remains.

The slender pinnacle of lava called Rocher d'Aiguilhe surges out of the plain and carries a lovely 11th century oratory, a miracle of medieval building skill. Rocher Corneille supports the 16m high statue of Notre Dame de France, gold paint and all, made out of 213 Russian cannon captured at Sebastopol. 19th century vulgarity at its most blatant!

*   *   *

Lace-making, Le Puy

After Le Puy, there are two pleasant little riverside resorts, Goudet and Arlempdes, reached through tightly winding valleys. Arlempdes sits above the gorge of the infant Loire, and has the obligatory ruined castle on basalt rocks. The river makes its way into Ardèche to curve to its source on the far side of Gerbier de Jonc, a bleak hill of 1,551m altitude. The departmental boundary between Haute-Loire and Ardèche runs over the summit of Mont Mézenc (1,753m), the watershed of Atlantic and Mediterranean. On the Haute-Loire side, it is a round, bald and featureless dead volcano — George Sand was here and described the scene in her *Le Marquis de Villemer* — with a few scattered

134

Approach to Pradelles in the high Cèvennes

farmsteads, the turf cropped by the Mézenc race of cattle. Botanically, Mézenc is noted for its alpines and medicinal herbs; the latter are sold at the fair of Ste. Eulalie on the first Sunday after 12th July, along with the Mezenc violets whose intense purple carpets the slopes in spring. Sheets of white narcissi appear in June, while the great botanical prize — to be photographed only — is the White Alpine Groundsel. It flowers between August and September, and the only other place where it is found is in the Eastern Pyrenees. It is the *Herbe de Mézenc*, *Senecio leucophyllus* in scientific nomenclature.

Midway between Le Puy and Mont Mézenc lies the *bourg* of Le Monastier-sur-Gazeille. As they are elsewhere in Velay, the houses are tall and grey and gaunt, as though remembering past suffering and deprivation. There is no mistaking that it is a place of literary pilgrimage. A large placard at each end of Le Monastier tells you so. A carved stone outside the Post Office speaks of the event. For it was from here on 22nd September, 1878, that R.L. Stevenson set out with his immortal donkey Modéstine for a month of *Travels with a Donkey in the Cévennes*. Just inside the Hôtel de Ville — a peeling, reverberating 18th century building whose walls are plastered with official notices of every kind — the R.L. Stevenson Club of Edinburgh has presented the town with a wall diagram of his route and photographs of a few places he passed through.

It is not easy to follow his track, though the *Syndicat d'Initiative* provides a map, and part of the route has been marked. The lazy way is to take the nearest metalled roads. You can get to Goudet and Château Beaufort, Ussel and Le

La Chaise-Dieu

Bouchet-St. Nicolas his journey mentions. At the latter, the inn he stayed at was still standing a few years ago, although falling into decay. Pradelles was Stevenson's last place of call in Haute-Loire before he goaded Modéstine on towards Langogne and the Cévennes.

Re-reading the *Travels,* I find myself slightly shocked that they were written barely a century ago. The conditions he describes fit the 18th century better.

* * *

To enter Haute-Loire by N106 from Arlanc brings one quickly to La Chaise-Dieu, where stands another great religious monument of Velay. *Casa Dei,* 'the House of God' lies high on exposed pastures at 1,082m. The first Benedictine abbey was founded here in 1043 by St. Robert of Aurillac. The present church was begun in the 14th century by a monk of La Chaise-Dieu who had become Pope Clement VI; it was finished by his nephew who also became pope as Gregory XI. Sacked by Huguenots in 1562, burned out in 1695, the reconstruction started by Louis XIV was stopped by the Revolution, although the abbey had already suffered a long period of decadence before then.

Descriptions from the last century of this massive and sombre southern Gothic basilica speak of the filth and stench of the derelict place within, but long and patient reconstruction is resurrecting the former magnificence. The sheer towering bulk of the front façade dominates the puny buildings below, shops selling tourist gifts and — more invitingly — bottles of Verveine du Velay.

Inside, the chief things to see are the tomb of Clement VI; the elaborately carved 14th century choir-stalls (estimates vary as to their number, perhaps 156); the 16th century Flanders tapestries; the 15th century rood-screen. To my mind, the most arresting is a painted frieze, 26m long, on the exterior of the choir-screen. This is the *Danse macabre,* executed in ochre and grey distemper on a red base, in the 15th century. Following in the wake of Adam are pope, emperor, cardinal, king, patriarch, knight, archbishop, doctor, troubadour, peasant, friar, mother and child — every class of 15th century society. Each figure is attended by its shadow of death. In 1938, the composer, Arthur Honegger, came here and drew inspiration for his 'Dance of Death'.

At the back of the church is the square donjon, the Tour Clémentine, overlooking the cloister where schoolchildren play, a very discreet carpark, a row of attractive outbuildings in which is housed the *Historial* museum of waxworks. And a little unexpectedly, until I reminded myself of the altitude, an office where you can enrol for Nordic cross-country skiing.

Between La Chaise-Dieu and Le Puy, D13 branches right from N106 at the untidy Sembadel-Gare, where the single street seems littered with piles of sawn wood. It is a pleasant and quiet road, skirting the wooded Lac de Malaguet, and Allègre on a steep hillside. Long ago, the great feudal castle fell

Church of St. Robert of Aurillac, La Chaise-Dieu

down, save for two towers supporting between them, in mid-air, a length of machicolated stonework. From the south, it looks like an enormous fragment of Stonehenge towering over the village. Locally, it is known as the *potence d'Allègre*, 'the gallows of Allègre'.

D13 rejoins N106 at St. Paulien. This was the capital of the Vellavi tribe in alliance with Vercingetorix against Caesar, and was known as *Ruessio, Revessium* or *Ruessium*, through which passed the Roman road of *Via Bolena* linking Loire with Allier. It retained its importance as the place where St. Paulien, bishop of Velay in the 5th century, was buried. During the French Revolution, the town was renamed Velauve.

*   *   *

A third way into Haute-Loire is by the Clermont-Ferrand — Le Puy road, though it is worth while following the N9 in crossing the Alagnon river at Lempdes, so as to go through the Gorges d'Alagnon. Both road and railway twist for fifteen km through the deep, wooded and variedly sculpted cliffs as

Cloister gallery, La Chaise-Dieu

Allègre

far as Le Babory-de-Blesle. A secondary road leads west to one of the conspicuously charming villages of Auvergne, Blesle. It lies in a protecting valley where two streams meet, and you move from one part of the graceful little town to another by small bridges. A Benedictine nunnery was founded here — *Blasilia*, as it was then — in 870, and for long the Mother Superior held feudal rights over the *bourg*. Part of the abbey church of St. Pierre dates from the 10th century, but the main body is Romanesque. A marble altar is thought to be the one presented to the founder of the nunnery, Ermengarde, wife of the Count of Auvergne, by the pope in 865. If the date is correct, it would have been Pope Nicholas I, and not one of the four Sergius popes, as the *Guide Bleu* states.

An unusual amount of decorative carving adorns St. Pierre; stone carvings on the portal and capitals, wood carving on the misericord seats of the choir-stalls. The story behind misericord seat carvings in general is a curious one. As clerics in the Middle Ages were obliged to stand through very lengthy offices both day and night, the physical strain fell hard on the elderly and infirm. A special indulgence — the misericord, which means 'pity' — allowed them to lean against an uplifted seat. After a time, the underside of these seats came to be carved, but purely religious themes were taboo because it was the priest's rump which came in contact with that part of the seat. Consequently, the carvings depicted ordinary activities; sometimes the carver had his bit of fun; occasionally he was downright lewd.

St. Pierre's treasury has a variety of things. There are portraits of former abbesses; of the carved figures, that of an 11th century Christ in wood is outstanding.

A cross-country road leads from Blesle to Brioude which possesses Auvergne's largest Romanesque church, considerably restored. The basilica of St. Julien was erected in the 11th and 12th centuries on the spot where the legionary Julien was martyred in 304. Its importance as a halting-place for pilgrims going to Spain is confirmed by the marble statue of St. James of Compostella in the north porch. It is possible to walk all round the outside of the majestic building.

Inside, Romanesque paintings were brought to light in 1957 in the Chapel of St. Michel and in the gallery of the narthex. One can see Christ Pantocrator, and Hell ruled over by a large green dragon, all done in sombre colours. Here is another 'Virgin with a Bird' (we met the other at Riom), gilded, 15th century, and rather more naive than the Riom carving.

But two figures are of more than passing interest. One is the 14th century statue of the Virgin in Childbirth — surely a rarely treated subject; the other is the Leprous Christ, also 14th century, in polychrome wood, from the one-time leper-house of Bajasse, perhaps carved by an inmate with all the knowledge of suffering the disease entailed.

Anyone wanting to see another Romanesque building in the vicinity should make for Lavaudieu on the Senouire stream in whose gentle valley are the remains of an 11th century Benedictine abbey. 14th century frescoes were uncovered in the nave in 1967, and the restored cloister, too, is a delight; it is the only one in Auvergne to have remained intact. Above the stonework is a wooden storey. Yet another fresco — a 13th century Virgin in Majesty — has been revealed in the chapter house.

Domeyrat down the road has a little Romanesque church, not noteworthy

architecturally, but it does contain a wood carving of 1503 of St. John the Baptist's head on a salver.

After Paulhaguet, on D51, comes the 18th century Château Chavaniac-Lafayette where General La Fayette was born in 1757, and which now contains a museum. The main road to Le Puy is met up with soon after.

*   *   *

All this may have concentrated too much on the ecclesiastical. Those who prefer riverine scenery can turn off at Vieille-Brioude and take the road that clings for many miles to the Allier. For the first ten km along N585 there is virtually no village. Opposite Villeneuve-sur-Allier stands the ruined castle of St. Ilpize high over the river. Lavoûte-Chilhac, with a few hundred inhabitants, seems almost large; it has a beautiful medieval bridge. St. Cirgues, next door, has a curious octagonal belfry with a curved stone spire above its tiny 13th century church. Chilhac sits atop a flat lump of phonolithic rock whose prisms, the geologists say, are exceptionally large.

Hamlet succeeds hamlet and the valley widens at the town of Langeac. You cross the St. Flour-Le Puy road, and as the valley narrows again and becomes prettier, it is worth while to swing into little Chanteuges where there are the remains of an abbey-church, and the view from its promontory above both Allier and Desges is fine. You must cross to St. Arcons-d'Allier to keep close to the river, and follow D48 to Prades and Monistrol-d'Allier, both little riverside resorts, the latter high above the gorge.

After Alleyras is Chapeauroux (upstream are vestiges of a Roman bridge); then the last cluster of houses at St. Médard where the road deserts the river. Either you must take the main N88 that swings back towards Le Puy, or a minor road to Pradelles. The Allier goes on by itself, separating Lozère from Ardeche in Stevenson country, before rising near La Bastide-Puylaurent.

Cloisters at Lavadieu

14

CANTAL

Cantal: first impressions flood the memory. I see grey roads winding in gentle ascent through miles of clean turf. Broad-horned Salers cattle, whose mahogany colour matches the soil. They graze on turf carpeting mahogany soil. Fresh molehills push upturned Christmas puddings of mahogany earth in an unsteady scattering across the green baize.

Mid-morning; the passage of motorists is constantly barred by cattle. Even hustling van drivers seem positively happy to wait and give the pride of Cantal right of way. At one place, the herd is large and cumbersome, and men with staves steer the beasts with taps and shouts. A cowherd gives me a wide-armed wave to point to our escape route, the back way through the village, a mud track of animal smells expanding into the waxing morning warmth. At another place, a little troupe of swinging udders gallops in single file along the roadside. Elsewhere, a small flock of goats leads a sedate line of cattle. At their head stumps a squat, straw-hatted, black-dressed woman, the archetypal pastoral Auvergnate.

Cattle and Cantal; Cantal and cheese. Glyn Daniel has observed that Cantal cheese is 'so reminiscent of Caerphilly and Wensleydale'.

In September, the greensward is suffused with a gentle flush of lilac-blue — tens of thousands of autumn crocus, petals thrown wide for a brief embrace with the sun.

Horizons are bold and reduced almost to abstract pictorial essentials. Especially do I see the expanse of short turf from the high vantage place of a south-facing bedroom, or from the huge picture-window, of Hôtel Europe in St. Flour, at sunrise. Shadows are elongated; each cow becomes a giraffe. The smallest hillock-nest of yellow ants becomes an image of the grassy cone of Mont Mézenc. The turf is the green coat over the flesh on the powerful frame of some inert, enormous animal.

*   *   *

One road into Cantal from Puy-de-Dôme is the main N9 which has worked its way through the Gorges d'Alagnon to Massiac, with St. Flour another thirty

La Place, Salers, Cantal

kilometres away over the Col de la Fageole (1,104m). Another, more attractive route, is from Besse-en-Chandesse to Condat, and a choice between N679 through Marcenat and Allanche, or the narrow D16 and Murat.

Or, coming from Bort-les-Orgues, you may take either the Rhue valley and its gorge to Condat, or else the Antignac to Riom-ès-Montagne road, almost as far as the peak of Puy Mary, where the St. Flour road swings eastwards over the Col de Serre (1,364m) to Murat.

This northwest corner of Cantal is for relishing a restful, simple landscape, harmonious villages, and the atmosphere of rural hotels. Champs-sur-Tarentaine, Antignac, Saignes, Ydes, Condat, Chastel-Marlhac, Menet, Apchon, Cheylade come to mind as having these qualities. There are villages with Romanesque churches; hamlets with Gallo-Roman ruins (Jallaniac, Auteroche and Cotteughe, for instance); castles at Chastanat, Cheyrousse, Saignes, Auzers. Moussages has a splendid view across to the high peaks of Cantal; more organ-pipe rocks at Valette and Milhac; the scattered lakes, streams and waterfalls. Hereabouts is a week's worth of exploration, though paradoxically, the major town, Riom-ès-Montagne, in spite of its church, is untidily banal.

At the approaches to the Monts du Cantal drama creeps in to the landscape. West of the ruined volcanic massif are popular resorts: Mauriac, Anglards-de-Salers, St. Bonnet-de-Salers, and Salers itself.

Salers is a satisfying place, high above the valley of the Maronne, a market town for cattle and cheese. Its 15th and 16th century homogeneity puts one in mind of a smaller Riom (the Puy-de-Dôme Riom, that is) — elegant town houses of judges and lawyers (for Salers became a bailiwick until the Revolu-

La Route de Salers, Puy Mary, Cantal

Le Puy Mary

tion). At its heart is the Grande-Place or, more correctly, Place Tyssandier-d'Escous, the name of the man who first bred the Salers race of cattle and whose bust is in the square. Like Riom, several elegant, dark-walled, turretted and emblazoned bourgeois mansions line the square and streets that lead towards the wide views, for Salers is 951m above sea-level. Gateways penetrate the remains of the ramparts which had been put up after the English and the freebooters had pillaged the place in the Middle Ages. Some of the *hôtels* can be visited. Maison de Bargues is one, while Maison des Templiers is the folklore and ethnology museum of Salers.

Puy Mary is a spectacular high point. From Salers, the direct route to it is N680 above the curving escarpment that sweeps down to the Maronne river. At Col de Néronne, the peak of Puy Violent (1,592m) rears across the valley, a dramatic shape and name. The road enters the Falgoux valley. On the right of the road is a restored barn, the Maison de la Forêt, a museum where techniques and human aspects of forest management are explained.

The Cirque de Falgoux, a majestic basin of meadows and pine trees, rises steadily until, with a sudden steep ascent, the Pas de Peyrol (1,589m) is reached. This is a popular stopping place from which to survey the peaks. From here it is a short, steep half-hour walk to the top of Puy Mary (1,787m). 'Proud Puy Mary', wrote the Cantalian poet, Arsène Vermenouze, 'this episcopal colossus thrusting the horns of its mitre into the sky'. There are, indeed, twin peaks. On one is the *table d'orientation;* on the other an iron cross.

The return to Salers follows down the Cirque de Falgoux again until a right turn takes the long, broad Vallée du Falgoux and the Mars stream. Hamlets dot the valley; a castle here and there, and the small resort of Anglards-de-Salers, surrounded by pastures, eleven kilometres from Salers across the high plateau.

West of Salers and Mauriac is the boundary between Cantal and Corrèze, marked by the Dordogne river. Very little of this splendid stretch of river can be followed by road from the Cantal side. The road which more or less falls in with the valley runs southwards from Bort-les-Orgues on the Corrèze side. Nonetheless, some impressive Cantalian spots can be reached; in particular, the Barrage de l'Aigle, a great semi-circular piece of architecture, 90 metres deep and 290 metres across the river, over which the Mauriac-Chalvignac road goes.

South of Salers, N122 is a winding road which calls at St. Martin-Valmeroux, the bailiwick of Haute-Auvergne before Salers usurped the role in the 15th century. It, too, has a pleasant square surrounded by turretted 15th and 16th century mansions. Then St. Chamant, a little to one side of the main road, and St. Cernin. Both places have churches with especially attractive 15th and 16th century carved choir stalls. In St. Cernin, particularly, the misericord carvings are delightful: here a meditating monk; there a monk reading with spectacles perched on his nose; a praying woman; another dressing herself; a man playing a flute; another overcoming a lion.

To reach Tournemire, it is again necessary to digress from the main road. It is said that a Thorn from the Crown of Christ was brought back by Rigald de Tournemire in 1101 from the Crusade. In the now almost totally vanished castle of Tournemire, the *routier* leader, Aymerigot Marchez, was incarcerated in 1390. Nearby, Château d'Anjony rears its high keep and four towers, and lets visitors see over it.

N122 runs into Aurillac, the capital of Haute-Auvergne, with a population of 31,000. It has churches and museums; its history is long, and distinguished men have been born in or near to it. It is well endowed with hotels and restaurants. Yet it feels above all to be a commercial and industrial town where the manufacture of umbrellas and overshoes lends itself to rueful jokes about Aurillac's weather.

I suppose I must have pinned unjustifiable hopes on Aurillac, my mind half-consciously influenced by a little sketch map of France in Cyril Connolly's wartime book, *The Unquiet Grave.* With its centre in Périgord, the circle just included Aurillac. It was Connolly's Magic Circle, his charm against Group Man, a seductive but evanescent fantasy for a writer. Aurillac caters for Group Man as well as any other town, and is not greatly concerned with charms

The Barrage de l'Aigle

against that profitable industry. What is in its favour is its strategic position as an excursion centre, for two of Auvergne's finest scenic roads start (or finish) from Aurillac.

At its very doorstep is the famous *Route des Crêtes*. Local experts advise one to do the downhill run, as it were, from Puy Mary towards Aurillac; if you can pick a fine sunset, the pleasure is even greater.

D17 sets out from Puy Mary along the Vallée de Mandailles, the almost alpine valley of the infant Jordanne river as it flows through meadows and forests. This road joins the *Route des Crêtes* for a long and splendid descent along the ridge dividing Jordanne and Authre (the latter flowing into the Dordogne).

The other handsome route into Aurillac comes from Murat, one of a number of small holiday towns lining N126. Set on the steep sides of the Alagnon valley, Murat is graced with dignified old grey houses bearing the characteristic turrets or *tourelles* of the region.

At Le Lioran, the road goes over the col separating Puy Mary and Plomb du Cantal, at 1,855m the second highest peak in the Massif Central. Le Lioran and Super-Lioran play the dual role of summer and winter resorts; extensive meadows below and above the pine forests are used by skiers and walkers. This is probably one of the best walking districts in Auvergne, with an immense range of not-too-difficult summits to tackle, as well as easy walks through the meadows. The pastures are dotted with *burons*, and one, Buron de Belles-Aygues, has been fitted up to show visitors what the traditional cowherd's life was like. Non-walkers are taken almost to the summit of the Plomb du Cantal by cablecar from Super-Lioran.

In summer, the motorist can take a minor road out of Le Lioran to rejoin N126 further along. N126 itself bores through the col by a tunnel, dug in 1839 to avoid the traffic delays caused by snowdrifts. In spite of its age, the tunnel is still impressive, its ovoid vaults spanning eight metres, the ceiling seven metres high. Still deeper underground is the railway tunnel, excavated in 1868.

On the southern side, the road drops into the Cère valley. Thiézac is a pleasant centre from which to walk to the Malbec waterfall, impressive provided there has not been too long a period of drought; and it is possible to walk to the *Route des Crêtes,* meeting up with it at St. Cirque-de-Jordanne.

Vic-sur-Cère is the most cheerfully pretty holiday place, for all that it is a spa which treats anaemia, renal and other conditions. More turretted mansions are to be seen, particularly the 15th century *hôtel* of the Princes of Monaco. A popular excursion is to Pas de Cère, a gorge hollowed out of volcanic rock. Signs of prehistoric dwellings, called Fours de la Prade, have to be imagined rather than seen, while some gouged out rocks are known as the *Grottes des Anglais.* Those unsavoury 14th century English bandits again! Certainly, Vic-sur-Cère, like Salers, had fallen foul of them.

Side roads from Vic lead to a number of little hill villages with marvellous views and small hotels — Pailherols, Lacapelle-Barrès, Raulhac and Thérondels.

At the approaches to Aurillac, the valley widens. Pesteils might make a halting place for a glance at its much rebuilt castle (not the English alone, but Huguenots and Revolutionaries were at it). Outside, its tall, square 14th century keep is handsome; inside can be seen 17th century ceiling paintings, furniture and Aubusson tapestries, as well as 15th century chivalric frescoes in the donjon.

*   *   *

La Bourrée, St. Flour, Cantal

The river Cère edges further and further away from N126, gives Aurillac a wide berth, swings west to widen and become the 13km long reservoir of St. Etienne-Cantalès. At one end, the railway line crosses the reservoir, and at the other, a road crosses the vaulted mass of the concrete dam built during the 1939-45 war. The tree-lined lake is a major yachting centre, dotted with islets.

Laroquebrou lies on the further side of the reservoir, the good looks of its dominating, ruined castle marred by a giant statue of the Virgin, which could be called an error of judgement. Further west, the Cère and the railway cut through a wild gorge to pass into Correze.

*   *   *

Garabit Viaduct, Cantal

Where Cantal juts into Aveyron, south of Aurillac, the country changes somewhat from the clean, open highlands to a shelf of granite, still fairly high plateau-land, but scored by narrow, wooded valleys that tip towards the Aquitanian basin. This is La Châtaigneraie, the Chestnut Country — not Horse, but Sweet Chestnut, of high commercial value in southern Europe. If the *castanet* plantations have lost something of their erstwhile supremacy, the 'chestnut language' is still used. *Affachados* and *brasucade* are two ways of grilling fresh autumn chestnuts after they have been taken out of their prickly *pelous*; or *bajana* chestnut soup with milk and wine — words that indicate the basic importance of the nut in the diet of the past.

Within the triangle formed by the two main roads out of Aurillac into La Châtaigneraie, N122 to Figeac, and N120 to Espalion, is a thinly populated region of small roads, scattered hamlets, farms and streams. Montsalvy, Calvinet, Cayrols, Boisset and Maurs are of historical or architectural interest, and have pleasant hotels.

Most guidebooks brush aside the ruined chateaux or churches; you are left to come upon them by chance. Fargues, Roquemaure, Senezergues, Marmiesse, Lamothe, Naucase, Marcolès: castles that can be tracked down on the Michelin map, often only with difficulty. The guidebooks have nothing to say about ruined Château de Merle near Fournoulès, nor about the hamlet of Merle near St. Mamet-la-Salvetat. But surely there must be some story here to tell about that flamboyantly fanatical 16th century Protestant marauder, Captain Merle, Auvergne got to know so unpleasantly well? One must turn to Peter Gorham's book In searching out the byways of La Châtaigneraie, he throws light on some of these places (and others as well); his most delightful sketch is of Marcolès.

Montsalvy, at 800m, with gateways at each end of its Grande-Rue — the southern one goes underneath the château; market-town Calvinet, where local business is conducted in the large square, and is only twenty kilometres from the great monastery church of Conques; both are unpretentiously pleasant for a short stay.

The main centre is Maurs. The Michelin map marks it with a black circle, and it is a little old town cleanly encircled by a boulevard shaded by plane trees on the site of its old fortifications, above the river Rance. They like to call Maurs the beginning of the Cantal Riviera, where the Midi begins. True, the cool grey of a hundred *bourgs* in Auvergne gives way at Maurs (only 280m above sea-level) to reddish roof-tiles and a gaiety of pot plants. A busy place is Maurs, a market for chestnuts, cattle, hams and agriculture produce. In the church is the 13th century reliquary bust of St. Césaire, another strangely arresting figure of wood, covered with copper sheet, and stone encrusted, his flat, elongated hands upraised in benediction, eyes large and staring; the face is strong, more human, perhaps, than the bust at St. Nectaire.

*   *   *

Roads approaching St. Flour from the north give no hint of its dramatic position, 900m up, high over the Lander river. For they slide in along the Planèze
plateau, whereas if you come from Le Puy or Mende you see the bold escarpment of prismatic basalt columns supporting a town of 7,300 inhabitants and
the cathedral. Ville-Basse by the river is modern; Ville-Haute is where history
is expressed in the grey 15th and 16th century houses, close-pressed over narrow streets. You emerge suddenly into space in the main square, Place des
Armes, in which stands the externally sullen Gothic church, its heavy square
towers throwing aggressive morning shadows. The original Romanesque
church was badly designed and fell down in 1396. This 15th century edifice is
better inside, for it contains the 13th century (or a 15th century copy?) *Le Bon
Dieu Noir*, a noble and beautiful Christ in wood, and a simple lava-stone 15th
century Pièta.

Not far away is the Hôtel de Ville — the 17th century episcopal palace —
where the Musée de la Haute-Auvergne exhibits archaeological finds, and the
religious art and traditions of the region.

St. Flour is a stimulating (visually and climatically) hub from which many
excursions radiate. The one which takes in Garabit, the Truyère lake and
Chaudes-Aigues is the most worthwhile. The Garabit viaduct, one of Gustave
Eiffel's metal bridges, was completed in 1884, five years before he put up his
tower in Paris. His other bridge in Auvergne is at Rouzat, near Vichy, erected
in 1869. Garabit is a majestic single-span arch of metal across the river Truyère, with five metal pillars supporting the railway track. The road bridge for
N9 is a little further downstream. Beyond is the large reservoir dammed by the
six vaults of the Barrage de Grandval. D13 quits N9 from the south side of the
river, to wander agreeably southwest through Faverolles and Auriac to the
Belvédère de Mallet, the name of a village drowned with the filling of the reservoir in 1959. 15th to 18th century statues from the chapel of Mallet were res-
cued and placed in a modern church at the next village of Fridefont. The
statues' themes are religious, but one introduces a touch of folk art by depicting an angel, dressed in Auvergnat Sunday finery, ministering to St. Roche.

The road crosses the massive concrete dam to come within sight of a romantic, hill-top ruined castle, Château d'Alleuze, a veritable stage-set. The last
occupant was a *routier* who plundered the region. He was finally bought out by
the exasperated and impoverished Sanflorains who, to make sure the experience would never be repeated, destroyed the castle in 1390.

The Truyère is recrossed at Pont de Lanau near another dam, and Chaudes-
Aigues in its deep circle of hills is soon reached. Chaudes-Aigues means 'hot
waters', and hot waters there are in abundance. The hottest spring gushes out
at 82°C, and the waters, exploited by the Romans, are used in the treatment of
rheumatism. Not only that, three-quarters of the houses have constant hot
water and central heating. This domestic exploitation has gone on for 2,000
years; many of the conduits are still made of pinewood.

Chaudes-Aigues

155

Gradually the road enters rather bleaker country, as it makes its way to the tip where Cantal, Lozère and Aveyron meet at Puy de Gudette. Our last place of call is St. Urcize, a huddle of mostly 17th century grey buildings, although the *Gendarmerie* is older. The village clings round the squat and powerful little Romanesque church on the hilltop. Four bells are suspended in the rectangular bell-tower, open to all weathers — all characteristically Cantalian. An early 12th century building, it has an endearing cluster of apses round the chevet; Peter Gorham says this apsidal east end is the only one to survive in Cantal, a testimony to the remoteness of St. Urcize. It feels remote, though once it stood on the pilgrim route between the great churches of Le Puy and Conques, on the route to Santiago de Compostella. So it is perhaps no accident that the capitals in the apsidal chapels resemble those of Ste. Foy at Conques.

The prospect beyond is of the southermost volcanic hills of the Massif Central, the Aubrac. Keen, clear air, high grazing lands and the transhumant sheep trails that were laid down long before history — the *Drailles de l'Aubrac* and *Margeride* — like so much of the Auvergne we have visited, enduring.

156

BIBLIOGRAPHY

Auvergne falls a little awkwardly for users of guide books. *Auvergne et Centre* (Hachette, 1970), and Michelin Green Guide *Auvergne-Bourbonnais* (Pneu Michelin, current edition) both cover the *départements* of Allier, Puy-de-Dôme, Cantal and western Haute-Loire. For Haute-Loire's eastern segment one must turn to *Cévennes-Languedoc* (Hachette, 1970), and Michelin Green Guide *Vallée du Rhône-Vivarais-Lyonnais* (Pneu Michelin, current edition). The Hachette volumes are the more substantial and thorough; they and the Michelin Guides are in French.

BARING-GOULD, S. (1907), *A Book of the Cévennes*. John Long.

CAESAR (1972), *The Conquest of Gaul* (translated by S.A. Handford). Penguin Books.

CUNLIFFE, Barry (1975), *Rome and the Barbarians*. Bodley Head.

GOODERS, John (1970), *Where to watch Birds in Britain and Europe*. André Deutsch.

GORHAM, Peter (1975), *Portrait of the Auvergne*. Robert Hale.

HATT, Jean-Jacques (1970), *The Ancient Civilisations of Celts and Gallo-Romans* (translated by James Hogarth). Barrie & Jenkins.

MORGAN, Bryan (1962), *Fastness of France: a book about the Massif Central*. Cleaver-Hume.

DE POLNAY, Peter (1952), *An Unfinished Journey to Southwestern France and Auvergne*. Allan Wingate.

REED, J.L. (1954), *Forests of France*. Faber & Faber.

ROWE, Vivian (1969), *The Loire*. Eyre & Spottiswoode.

STERNE, Laurence (1967), *A Sentimental Journey through France and Italy*. Penguin Books.

STEVENSON, R.L. (1919), *Travels with a Donkey in the Cévennes*. Chatto & Windus.

WHITE, Freda (1964), *West of the Rhône: Languedoc, Roussillon, the Massif Central*. Faber & Faber.

YOUNG, Arthur (1913), *Travels in France during the Years 1787, 1788, 1789*. G. Bell.

INDEX

Agonges 108
Ajalbert, Jean (1863-1947) 13
Alagnon 17
Allanche 17
Allier 11, 14, 17, 32, 50, 64, 83, 104-115
Allier, River 15, 16, 17, 19, 75, 84
Ambert 14, 64
Antignac 32
Aquitaine 14, 55
Ardeche 14, 15
Arlempdes 134
Auberges Rural 32
Aurillac 14, 53, 64, 93, 148-150
Auvergne, Pierre d' 95
Aveyron 11, 15, 50

Balzac 44
Barbier, Aristide 100
Barrès, Maurice 44
Beaujolais 14
Belliac 93
Berry 14
Besbre Valley 109
Bessé-en-Chandesse 73
Blesle 140-141
Bort-les-Orgues 128
Bourbon, House of 55, 105
Bourbon-l'Archambault 14, 43, 44, 48,
    55, 106
bourrée, the 71
Bourboule, La 14, 45
Brioude 14, 17, 53, 55, 141
Burgundy 11, 16, 49
Cantal 11, 14, 16, 22, 25, 32, 69, 70, 75, 82,
    144-156

Cévennes 14, 22
Chaise-Dieu, La 14, 137
Chamalières 43
Chambon-du-Lac 84, 124
Champagnac-les-Mines 64
Champeix 53
Chantelle 110
Chanteuges 143
Chardin, Pierre Teilhard de 97, 102
Charlemagne 53, 81
Chasteloy 82
Châtaigneraie, La 22
Châteauneuf-les-Bains 47
Châtel-de-Neuve 17
Châteldon 88, 116
Châtel-Guyon 14, 47
Chaudes-Aigues 14, 47
Cher, River 15
Clermont-Ferrand 12, 14, 16, 21, 53, 5
    59, 61, 63, 73, 74, 77, 78, 81, 84, 91,
    100, 117
Clovis 53
Colbert, Jean-Baptiste 64
Commentry 64
Condat-en-Féniers 67
Couze 17

Daubrée, Edouard 100
Dordogne, River 15, 128, 148
Dore, River 15, 17, 116
Doumer, Paul 99

Edward, the Black Prince 56
Eiffel, Alexandre Gustave 110-111, 15⁄

Fayette, Marquis de La 98
Foret de Tronçaus 113
Forez 14, 22
France Accueil 32
France, Anatole 44
Froissart, Jean 58

Gannat 53
Gautier, Théophile 44
Gerbert 93
Gergovie 51, 52, 53, 89
Gévaudan 14
Glozel 53, 111
Goncourt brothers 44
Gooders, John 23, 24
Goudet 134
Grand-Genévrier, Le 39
Gregory of Tours 93
Guesclin, Bertrand du 56

Haute-Loire 11, 14, 16, 19, 32, 63, 69, 75
Hèrault, River 15
Huriel 115

Issoire 14, 17, 78, 82, 124

Jailhac 86
Jaligny-sur-Besbre 63, 109
Jenzat 110
Joan of Arc 56

Langeac 17, 143
Lapalisse 14
Laval, Pierre 61, 87, 116
Lavoûte-sur-Loire 130
Lavaudieu 141
Laroquebrou 151
Lezoux 52, 53
Limagne 16, 63
Limousin 14
Lioran-Laveissiere Le 48
Logis de France 32
Loire, River 15, 16
Lot, River 15
Loubaresse 74
Lyon 16

Mapotel 34
Maringues 17
Marsat 73
Massif Central 11, 14, 21-23, 49
Maupassant, Guy de 44
Mauriac 14, 37, 73, 84
Maurs 22, 153
Merle, Captain 59, 153
Michelet, Jules 12
Michelin, André 100
Michelin Guide 34
Monastier-sur-Gazeille 135
Mont Dore, Le 14, 18, 46
Monts de la Madeleine 19, 22, 111, 113
Montluçichy 14
Montluçon 64, 72
Mont Mouchet 62
Moulins 14, 53, 55, 63, 105, 106
Murat 37
Murol 53

Napoleon 44
Neris 43, 48, 53, 114-115

Olliergues 119
Orcival 73, 78

Pailherols 32
*Parc Naturel Régional des Volcans
d'Auvergne* 25-27
Pascal, Blaise 96-97
Peirols, Hughes de 95
Périgord 14
Puy-de-Dôme 11, 14, 16, 18, 32, 63, 69,
82, 84, 116-128
Puy-en-Velay, Le 130-131
Puy, Le 14, 53

Quercy 14

Riom 14, 63, 64, 73, 74, 121
Richard Coeur-de-Lion 55, 95
Roch, Nicolas Sébastien 97
Romains, Jules 101
Rouergue 14
Royat 14, 48

Saignes 32
Sand, George 44, 90, 117, 134
Salers 146-147
Saugues 73
Ségalas 14
Sévigne, Madame de 44, 71
Sidonius Appollinaris 40-41, 91
Sioule, River 15, 17
Souvigny 108-109
Stevenson, Robert Louis 32, 136
St. Austremoine 53, 91, 122
St. Cernin 148
St. Chamant 148
St. Eloy-les-Mines 14
St. Flour 14, 23, 48, 50, 53, 62, 154
St. Martin-Valmeroux 148
St. Menoux 108
St. Nectaire 14, 48, 50, 78, 86, 124
St. Paulien 139
St. Pourçain-sur-Sioule 14, 41, 110
St. Yorre 64

Taleyrand 44
Tarn, River 15

Tazieff, Haroun 25
Thiers 14, 53, 63, 116-117
Tournemire 148
Truyère, River 15
Turenne, Marshal 97

Ussel-d'Allier 110

Varennes 63, 64
Védrines-Saint-Loup 32
Velay 14, 82, 129
Vercingétorix 51, 52, 89, 121, 139
Vertolaye 64
Veurdre, Le 104
Viaur, River 15
Vichy 17, 44, 45, 46, 61-62, 63
Vic, Pierre de 95
Vic-sur-Cère 37, 150
Vivarais 14
Vix 49
Volvic 77

Yssingeaux 14, 37